Playing with Fire

Feminist Thought and Activism Through Seven Lives in India

Playing with Fire

Feminist Thought and Activism Through Seven Lives in India

Sangtin Writers:
Anupamlata, Ramsheela, Reshma Ansari, Richa Nagar, Richa Singh, Shashi Vaish, Shashibala, Surbala and Vibha Bajpayee

zubaan

An Imprint of Kali for Women

Playing with Fire: Feminist Thought and Activism Through Seven Lives in India
Anupamlata, Ramsheela, Reshma Ansari, Richa Nagar, Richa Singh, Shashi Vaish, Shashibala, Surbala and Vibha Bajpayee

Published 2006 by
Zubaan, an imprint of Kali for Women
K-92, First Floor,
Hauz Khas Enclave,
New Delhi – 10016, INDIA
Email: zubaanwbooks@vsnl.net and contact@zubaanbooks.com
Website: www.zubaanbooks.com

Royalties due to the authors will go to the organization, Sangtin.

Zubaan is an independent feminist publishing house based in New Delhi, India, with a strong academic and general list. It was set up as an imprint of the well known feminist house Kali for Women, and carries forward Kali's tradition of publishing world quality books to high editorial and production standards. "Zubaan" means tongue, voice, language, speech in Hindustani. Zubaan is a non-profit publisher, working in the areas of the humanities, social sciences, as well as in fiction, general non-fiction, and books for young adults that celebrate difference, diversity and equality, especially for and about the children of India and South Asia under its imprint - Young Zubaan.

ISBN 81 89013 68 8

Typeset at Print Services, B-17, Lajpat Nagar, Part II, New Delhi – 110024
Printed at Raj Press, R-3, Inderpuri, New Delhi – **110 012**

Acknowledgements

We have embraced many risks and undergone many hardships in writing this story of our collective journey. As we place these churnings of our minds and souls in your hands, we feel a peace and contentment we have not known before.

We are grateful to all those friends and institutions whose long companionship gave us the ideas, vision, and strength to undertake this work, and all the signatories on our petition who helped us to continue our journey.

Urvashi Butalia, Bandhu Kushawarti, M. J. Maynes, Shruti Tambe, Ganesh Visputay, Rajendra Yadav, and members of the Women's Studies Center at the University of Pune and the Centre for the Study of Regional Development at the Jawaharlal Nehru University, New Delhi gave early encouragement to *Sangtin Yatra*. Without the intellectual and political support that we received from various quarters in India and the U.S. between April 2004 and April 2005, Sangtin Yatra might have ended before we could have claimed to play with fire. While it is not possible to mention each person by name, we would like to thankfully acknowledge the critical support and ideas we received from Kshama Awasthi, Bhashwati, Piya Chatterjee, Anil Chowdhury, Raymond Duvall, Sharilyn Geistfeld, Vaijayanti Gupta, Sangeeta Kamat, Amy Kaminsky, Cindi Katz, Krishna Kumar, Geeta Kumari, Chandra Talpade Mohanty, Sanat Mohanty, Sudha Nagavarapu, Reena

Pandey, Shahnaz Parveen, Mir Raza, Abdi Samatar, Naomi Scheman, Eric Sheppard, Ashwini Tambe and Raghu Tiwari.

James Bishara, David Faust, Jim Glassman, Gita Ramaswamy, Abdi Samatar and Edén Torres were among the first to read the initial translation of *Sangtin Yatra* and conversations with them and with Sister Concilia and Ram Sudhar Singh inspired us to create *Playing with Fire*. We are particularly indebted to eleven people who closely read the manuscript in whole or in part, and whose incisive comments and challenging questions from varied perspectives were invaluable in not only shaping the final form of the Introduction and Postscript, but also in helping us collectively reflect on the continuities and shifts in our ongoing journey and alliance: Urvashi Butalia, Jigna Desai, Cynthia Enloe, David Faust, Jim Glassman, Sangeeta Kamat, Helga Leitner, Naomi Scheman, Eric Sheppard, Amanda Swarr and Ashwini Tambe. We also thank participants in the Fall 2004 Gender, Space and Resistance seminar at the University of Minnesota who provided helpful critical commentary on three chapters, and Ron Aminzade and Joel Wainwright who shared key references on the politics of NGOs. We are grateful to Eric Baker for happily devoting part of his vacation in India on carefully reviewing the complete manuscript, and to Deeksha Nagar for her help with refining the Glossary.

Since March 2002, the financial support for various segments of this journey has come from a Grant-in-aid of Research, Artistry and Scholarship; a McKnight Presidential Award; and a sabbatical supplement, all from the University of Minnesota; and a *saathiship* (fellowship for activists) from the Minnesota Chapter of the Association for India's Development.

In different ways, Babuji, Amma, David, Mukesh, Maa and Jamil have given pieces of their soul to this work and to this journey. We express our *dili shukriya* for all the ways in which they have helped to envision, inspire and fire this work – and to help us grow during times when we feared we might sink.

Anurag, Anuradha, Richu, Kirti, Khushnuma, Neelam, Partha, Pushkar, Pooja, Vipin, Manu, Madhukar, Medha, Mohammed Zeeshan, Mohammad Shadab, Mohammad Shahid, Rahnuma, Vartika, Shahina, Sachin and Sarthak not only lived without us from several days to several months, but they also became a support for us and for each other. To these daughters and sons we express our heart-felt thanks. A significant amount of the time, energy and care that they were entitled to, was devoted to the undertaking of this work

The Authors' Collective

to those women
of Sitapur District
who gave us the courage and inspiration
to undertake this journey...

Contents

PART I

INTRODUCTION

Richa Nagar

Playing with Fire: A Collective Journey Across Borders

> If we have learned anything about anthropology's encounter with colonialism, the question is not really whether anthropologists can represent people better, but whether we can be accountable to people's own struggles for self-representation and self-determination.
>
> — Kamala Visweswaran, *Fictions of Feminist Ethnography*

> [Conscientizacion] is a consciousness of [our] own political positions in the world and what that means in terms of finding ways to create change . . . [A] critical look at one's own suffering and the ability to feel empathy may be required for making this transition from one identity to another.
>
> —Edén E. Torres, *Chicana Without Apology*

How does one tell the story of a journey undertaken by nine women? And how does one try to capture the meanings of such a journey when it is continuously evolving and unfolding, sometimes in the face of intense backlash? *Playing with Fire* seeks to tell that story as a chorus where nine travelers from varied socio-political locations self-reflexively merge their voices to seek answers to a set of shared concerns. Although these travelers inhabit different and unequal worlds in many ways, we are bound together by a shared intellectual and political agenda—and by a passion to envision and rebuild our interconnected worlds, even if such a project involves playing with fire.

Playing with Fire is set primarily in Uttar Pradesh (U.P.), the most populous state of India, one that has been influential in the country's political life. Stretching across the Gangetic plain, U.P. is mainly an agricultural state. As a state ranking low in conventional measures of economic and human development, U.P. has been the target of numerous 'development' initiatives, many of which are funded, at least in part, by the state or central government and operated by non-governmental organizations (NGOs). NGO projects run the gamut from sectoral initiatives in water or agriculture to programs for education or women's empowerment. At the centre of our story are two such organizations that seek to empower rural women in the Sitapur district of U.P.—Sangtin and Nari Samata Yojana (NSY). Sangtin is a small organization that the eight activists who co-authored this book established in 1998 with and for rural women of Sitapur district. NSY is a pseudonym we deploy for a large government-sponsored women's organization in Sitapur, in which all the Sangtin members who co-authored this book have served as employees for varying lengths of time and in various positions since 1991.[1] With the exception of Sangtin, we use pseudonyms for NSY and all other women's NGO whose activities or events we discuss in *Playing with Fire*; our goal is not to launch criticisms against specific organizations or individuals but to grapple with complex and contradictory processes and hierarchies associated with donor-funded NGO work and visions of women's empowerment.

In this chorus of nine voices, seven belong to Anupamlata, Ramsheela, Reshma Ansari, Shashibala, Shashi Vaish, Surbala and Vibha Bajpayee— village-level NGO activists from diverse caste and religious backgrounds, who have worked as mobilizers in seventy villages of the Sitapur district. These seven women formed an alliance with each other; with Richa Singh, their co-worker and a district-level NGO activist; and with me, a teacher at the University of Minnesota.[2] We deploy reflexive activism and collective analysis of the lives and work of the seven village-level activists to articulate the nuanced intersectionality of caste, class, gender, religion and socio-spatial location, on the one hand, and the multivalent and hierarchical character of donor-driven women's empowerment, on the other. We mix and blur creative, academic and journalistic writing to critically explore the manner in which social hierarchies based on caste, class, religion and geographical location become central to understanding the interrelationships among women's empowerment, NGO work and the politics of knowledge production. Our goal is to reach anyone who might have some interest in understanding the long-term struggles that we have embraced—researchers, community-workers, NGO officials, practitioners in the realms of education and development, and those who are invested in (or disenchanted by) the notion of 'empowering the marginalized.'

Playing with Fire has emerged from *Sangtin Yatra*, a book in Hindi that the nine authors of this book published in India in March 2004. In Awadhi,[3] *sangtin* is a term of solidarity, of reciprocity, of enduring friendship among women; it is used by a woman to refer to her close female companion who sees her through the trials and tribulations of life. The word, *yatra*, in both Awadhi and Hindi, means journey. The title of our original Hindi book, *Sangtin Yatra* or a journey of *sangtins*, captures the essence of our collaboration, while also highlighting the name of the organization Sangtin, in whose name the authors want to continue the work of combining rigorous research, radical activism and creative writing.

The public release of *Sangtin Yatra* triggered an angry response from the state headquarters of NSY and the emergence of *Playing with Fire* is inevitably shaped by this controversy. To counter NSY's backlash, we had to step into the regional, national and international realm to gain support for our freedom of expression. Mobilizing supporters who do not read Hindi necessitated that the contents of *Sangtin Yatra* be made available in English. Furthermore, NSY's response as well as the encouragement from intellectuals, activists and NGO workers in and outside India, made us confident about *Sangtin Yatra's* ability to speak to important public debates involving NGOs, empowerment and 'poor women.' As the authors revised and updated the original *Sangtin Yatra* and transformed it into *Playing with Fire*, we fully recognized that no act of translation is without problems of voice, authority and representation, and that no act of publication comes without risks and consequences.[4] Yet, we feel that it is necessary for the insights and critiques of this journey to move across the borders of languages, communities, social spaces and institutions. We have chosen to embrace the risks posed by such border-crossings rather than maintaining the silences that *Sangtin Yatra* seeks to break. Hence, the title, *Playing with Fire*.

In a large measure, the significance of this collaboration is tightly interwoven with the labour process that went into the making of *Sangtin Yatra/Playing with Fire*, and the contradictory realities of a collective praxis that consciously aims to intervene in the discourse and politics of empowerment. This collaboration also suggests possibilities and limitations created by the strategy of writing and publishing locally and in the 'vernacular' (Hindi/Hindustani)[5], and of subsequently reaching out to national, global and English-speaking audiences. Sharing insights about key pieces of our process can productively contribute to the ongoing discussions—in a variety of institutions and settings—about why and how collaborative research and knowledge production can be imagined across geographical, socio-economic and institutional borders, and the ways in which questions of representation, voice, authority and privilege might be negotiated in the enacting of such an alliance.

The task of framing and translating this journey as one of its travellers—and also as the sole English speaker, academic and Non-Resident Indian in the group—certainly comes with immense material and symbolic privileges. It also comes with huge responsibilities: First and foremost, the responsibility to remain accountable to my collaborators who have trusted me to narrate our journey for readers in worlds far removed from their own; and second, the responsibility to the readers who want to understand the processes, dilemmas and challenges associated with our collaboration. But how does one frame a journey whose whole purpose is to not be framed by a single individual? Even though *Playing with Fire* is framed by my singular voice, what I narrate and analyse is an account of a process whose terms and priorities are set collectively in relation to the politics in which the activists are inserted. The process leading to the creation of *Sangtin Yatra*, and the journey that continues as a result of it are as critical for its authors as the text is, if not more. In this sense, questions about the meanings and relevance of *Sangtin Yatra* cannot be answered internally by any one of its travellers; the answers can emerge only in the context of activism and NGO work—the spaces where this effort evolved and where it seeks to spark energy and critical dialogues. In the Introduction and Postscript, I highlight and contextualize this bigger journey in which *Sangtin Yatra* marks a 'moment' of creation.

Before proceeding, a few words are in order about the use of the terms '*sangtins*,' 'autobiographers' and 'activists' in the Introduction and Postscript. Sangtin is the name of an organization created by rural women in the Mishrikh block of Sitapur district to work together for the socio-political and intellectual empowerment of themselves and their communities.[6] *Sangtin Yatra* was fired by a desire to imagine how this organization Sangtin could become a *sangtin*—or a close friend and companion—for the most marginalized women of Sitapur. At the same time, the very nature of *Sangtin Yatra* also made it an intense personal, intellectual and political journey through which nine collaborators became *sangtins*. These nine *sangtins* are synonymously referred to as 'the *sangtins*,' 'the authors,' and 'the collective.' To distinguish the *sangtins* from the seven village-level activists, whose diaries provided the nodal points for *Sangtin Yatra*, I use the terms, 'the diary-writers' or 'the autobiographers.' Finally, Richa Singh and the seven diary writers, all of whom are also co-workers and formal members of Sangtin, are referred to as 'the activists,' 'the group,' or 'the members of Sangtin.' I use the words 'we' to refer to the nine authors, and 'they' when I am alluding to the seven autobiographers or the eight members of Sangtin.[7]

Playing with Fire is divided into three parts. The present Introduction complements the first chapter of *Sangtin Yatra* by contextualizing and describing some of the key phases of this journey. The second part of the book, entitled 'A Journey of Sangtins,' contains six chapters that constitute the English version of *Sangtin Yatra*. We begin with the story of why and how we undertook this collaboration, and then share our discussion and analysis of the seven autobiographers' childhoods, adolescence and marriages; their political coming of age; and their triumphs and challenges as workers in women's NGOs. The sixth chapter reflects on the politics of NGO work, and how a desire to reshape these politics allows the collective to articulate our dreams for Sangtin.

The final section is a Postscript where I discuss NSY's backlash against *Sangtin Yatra* in relation to the politics of empowerment and NGO work, articulations of global and local feminisms, and globalization from below. I highlight how this journey enacts the theory and praxis of collaboration, while also seeking to shift dominant expectations about who can produce knowledge; the languages, genres and forms in which knowledges get produced; and how new knowledges gain relevance as they interact with different audiences and enable new kinds of socio-political interventions.

Placing the Collaboration

How did nine women become nine *sangtins*? Why and when did we choose to trust each other and travel together; to share our fears and anxieties; to dig out memories and secrets we had buried years ago? How did the collective identify the issues we want to fight for, and how did the activists come to risk their livelihoods and some of their closest relationships for that battle? These questions about building relationships and alliances cannot be 'uncovered' in a methodological vein as if they were transparent realities.[8] However, in discussing the issues of origins, process and intended audience, the first chapter of *Sangtin Yatra/Playing with Fire* establishes us as nine actors from diverse social, geographical and institutional locations, whose coming together in March 2002 was facilitated by two sets of common concerns which we came to name as the 'politics of knowledge production' and the 'NGOization of women's empowerment.'[9] We explain how we embarked on this journey and why the collective chose to focus the book on the lives of the seven village-level activists instead of nine *sangtins*.

In many ways, the concerns that pulled us together are similar to the concerns that are being raised by critics throughout the so-called third world.[10] At the same time, the place-specific context of Sitapur played an important role in shaping our engagements as well as the effects that those engagements were able to produce.

Sitapur district is located about ninety kilometres away from Lucknow, the capital of U.P. According to the 2001 census, approximately 3.6 million of U.P.'s 166 million people lived in the Sitapur district.[11] Comprising 19 blocks and spreading over an area of 5743 sq. km., one third of the total population of this district is classified as 'scheduled caste' (Dalits). Despite a significant presence of Muslims (17 per cent) and the dominance of electoral politics by Samajwadi Party and Bahujan Samaj Party, the district has witnessed a heavy influence of Bhartiya Janata Party in the years following the destruction of the Babri mosque in 1992. Although the glory of the Hindu goddess, Sita, is frequently invoked in this Hindutva-inflected district, it is perhaps equally well-known for being a centre for buying and selling of poor women brought from outside, as well as for heinous acts of violence against women. A recent study on district-level deprivation officially classifies Sitapur as one of the '69 most backward districts' of India.[12]

The close proximity to the state capital not only affects the electoral and communal politics in Sitapur, but it also makes this district an attractive backyard for various experiments in development schemes and NGO initiatives. While landlessness is not as acute as in other parts of U.P., a large number of Dalit men and women have been forced to find livelihoods in the informal sector of urban centres such as Lucknow and Kanpur, primarily as cycle-rickshaw pullers and domestic workers. Women and girls frequently work on farmland that is either owned or contracted by their own families; they seldom work as wage labourers for others. A significant number of women and girls are also employed by middle people to do piecework making *bidis* or as *chikankari* embroiderers or weavers, for urban-based merchants under exploitative conditions and in the absence of any unions.

Although not very far from the newly formed hill-state of Uttaranchal—a fertile ground for the growth of various people's movements—Sitapur has largely remained untouched by periodic waves of socialist, workers' or peasants' movements, or activism against state-aided communalism in the post-independence period. This is particularly surprising when one considers the presence of the large work force in the sugar mills, plywood factories and *dari* weaving industry. The district also remained mostly unmarked by the influence of the women's movement in the 1970s and 1980s, although women's rights and empowerment were often alluded to in government documents and programmes.[13]

After the mid-1990s, things began to change with the appearance of donor-funded women's NGOs in the district. For the eight activists undertaking Sangtin Yatra, the arrival in 1996 of NSY marked a new beginning in their lives. A programme for the empowerment of rural women from marginalized sections, NSY-Sitapur was initially funded by the World Bank and implemented through the Human Resources and Development Ministry of the Government of India. The programme follows the principle of geographical decentralization. It is headquartered at the state level but works through district-level offices so that rural activists working at the village level can create spaces for women in their communities to define their own priorities and strategies for how they want to mobilize and address the problems that seem most urgent to them.

NSY often encourages its village-level workers to register their own organization under another name so that the work of women's empowerment may continue after the time-bound funded programme of NSY withdraws from the district.[14] Thus, the Sitapur branch of NSY, U.P. is the parent organization from which Sangtin has emerged. To the extent that NSY was already 'rolling-back' from Mishrikh, the part of Sitapur where Sangtin operates, and because the collective's objective was to imagine the future of Sangtin by critically reflecting on the activists' previous work, we perceived *Sangtin Yatra* as being complementary rather than oppositional to NSY's goals.

A Collective Methodology

Sangtin Yatra/Playing with Fire has emerged from a collectively produced methodology, where autobiographical writing and discussions of those writings became tools through which we built our analysis and critique of societal structures and processes —ranging from the very personal to the global. At all times, the momentum for this work came from the collective's aim to envision the future directions of Sangtin, and its belief that these future directions would be beset with the same difficulties that we were critiquing unless we could honestly grapple with the silences and barriers that stood in our own midst.

Our reflexive analysis evolved as a step-by-step process, where the autobiographers began by writing on their childhoods, adolescence and sexuality. These accounts became the starting points to interrogate different meanings of poverty, hunger, privilege and oppression, and to critically analyse personal dynamics of casteism, communalism and elitism in the autobiographers' own lives, among ourselves, and in the organizations where the activists worked. Finally, we grappled with the nuances of representation, hierarchy and ownership of intellectual work within changing structures of NGOs.

The topics of the autobiographical diary writing were collectively determined, and the discussions sparked by diaries became spaces where issues of voice, power, silences—and silencing—were constantly raised with respect to the differences and conflicts within the collective, as well as with respect to the politics of caste, class, gender, communalism and development NGOs that stretched beyond us. Each phase of the journey has been marked by shared decision-making on a range of issues, for example: (a) the 'whys' and 'hows' of diary writing; (b) rules pertaining to the sharing of diaries and collective discussions; (c) publishing a book based on the discussions; (d) the writing, sharing and revising by collaborators across geographical boundaries; (e) public release function and distribution of the Hindi book; (f) expenses involved in each stage; (g) translations of *Sangtin Yatra* into English and South Asian languages; (h) who shall publish, how the authors shall be named, the royalties allocated, and the contracts signed for *Playing with Fire;* (i) the complete contents of *Playing with Fire* and the second Hindi edition of *Sangtin Yatra* [15] and (j) the future projects that Sangtin is undertaking in the light of this journey.

The Labour Process

The collective labour process that created *Sangtin Yatra/Playing with Fire* unfolded over the course of 34 months. We began in March 2002 with conversations about the activists' long–term dream of establishing Sangtin as an effective organization in the lives of the poorest women in Sitapur district and the manner in which autobiographical narratives and group reflections of their own lives and work could help that process. After nine months of discussion over letters, emails and meetings, we gathered in December 2002 to determine the specific aims, focus, methods, schedule and codes of conduct by which narratives were going to be written and shared. In working out these details, all of us experimented with diary writing and discussion to see how the process might unfold and to develop the steps that would ensure that the sharing and discussion of the narratives happened within a format in which all voices were heard more or less equally.

Since one of the goals from the outset was to intervene in the politics of knowledge production, the eight activists wished to learn everything that counted as 'research' and 'documentation' in NGO work, but which was often done on, about or for their work by 'more skilled experts' who came from outside. The tape recorder was a symbol of this expertise, and tape recording could also be used as required by the collective in our own journey. I worked with the eight members of Sangtin as they learned to interview each other, operate a tape recorder, and transcribe recorded material.

During the next six months, Vibha Bajpayee, Surbala, Shashi Vaish, Shashibala, Reshma Ansari, Ramsheela and Anupamlata worked on five topically focused autobiographical narratives about their childhood, adolescence and marriage, their initial introduction to the world of women's NGOs, and the struggles they got involved in as NGO activists in their homes and communities. They met with each other and Richa Singh for regular discussions of these narratives while I communicated with the group after each discussion by phone from Minnesota.

The next phase commenced in July 2003 when I rejoined the group during my sabbatical year. During this time, we revisited what we had learned from the journey thus far. The discussions on complexities of caste, gender and poverty quickly spilled from the sphere of personal lives into the realms of NGOization, development politics and social movements—topics that were largely absent in the initial phase of diary writing. Long conversations ensued on a number of topics—e.g., transparency and accountability in NGO-based development, water crisis in rural India, increasing numbers of suicides by Indian peasants, communalism and electoral politics in U.P., and the ways in which impoverishment of the rural communities was connected with gendered and caste-based violence as well as with economic policies propagated by the World Trade Organization, the World Bank and the International Monetary Fund. The collective became interested in understanding the changing nature of money trails in various women's organizations and their linkages with the ways empowerment is measured and evaluated by donor-funded NGOs. For example, we considered how the involvement of the World Bank in NSY (previously supported primarily by the Royal Dutch Government) had overlapped with critical programmatic shifts where more qualitative 'measurements' of empowerment have given way to an expansion of the programme's scale of operation and a greater preoccupation with statistics and standardization of 'successful' strategies.

In addition, the US-led invasion of Iraq became a prominent subject of concern in the above discussions and the group wanted me to play an active role in helping them learn first about US foreign policy in the Middle East and South Asia, and then about race politics in the U.S. and South Africa.[16] Focused discussions on issues of sexual desires and same-sex sexuality also happened for the first time at this point. The passionate engagement of the group with all these topics prompted us to reflect and write about these in our diaries for forty minutes after each discussion, and return again to share our thoughts.

At this juncture, the collective felt that in order to honour our own accountability to Sangtin, we should compile our discussions in a form that could be shared with other fellow activists and members of Sangtin. When Richa Singh and I compiled the first set of notes on childhood and Anupamlata read them aloud in a group discussion, each of us felt overwhelmed by what we had been able to articulate. Surbala and Shashibala wondered aloud, 'What would happen if our stories could replace the stories of Sita and Jhansi ki Rani in our school text-books?' Suddenly, the collective was struck by the power of its own creation. The question raised by Surbala and Shashibala crystallized in the autobiographers a desire to claim authorship of their own lives and struggles, and culminated in the decision to publish *Sangtin Yatra*.

Everyone participated in determining what the book should look like, which stories and discussion points should appear in the book and which should not; and which issues needed further discussion and fleshing out before incorporation into the book. This process sometimes triggered memories and emotions that drew our attention to issues we had not talked about previously. For example, the sensitive topic of whether and how the hunger of two poor girls from different locations in the caste ladder could be compared to each other first came up in this new round of discussions. Revisiting childhood and deprivation subsequently triggered memories of infants and children that four of the autobiographers had lost due to disease, malnutrition, or lack of adequate health care infrastructure in rural areas, as well as memories of the ways in which two autobiographers were subjected to practices of untouchability when they delivered their babies. Recollection and reflection on these events soon after having discussed the bigger picture of how development politics works, helped us to formulate more nuanced and multilayered understandings of how intersecting forms of structural violence play out on bodies marked by gender, caste and religion.

Once all the authors took critical decisions about the contents and structure of the book in August 2003, Richa Singh and I plunged ourselves into preparing drafts of each chapter. Richa Singh focused on outlining the details of the stories that the authors had collectively decided to include, making sure that all the key points of tension, reflections and debate were captured by the text we were creating. My energies were focused on writing, sharing and redrafting every piece of the text until it met with full satisfaction and approval from the other eight authors. This process gave each member of the collective a sense of ownership of the words and thoughts that were being written, discussed, negotiated, revised and re-revised.

It took six months of intensive writing to produce the first complete draft of *Sangtin Yatra*, and during two of these months I was located in the U.S. once again. The geographical distance made it necessary for us to figure out ways to communicate over long distance—not simply to complete the project at hand, but also to sustain and grow a long-term alliance. As a first step, I learned to type in Hindi while Richa Singh (who already knew how to type in Hindi) learned to use a computer and email. We discovered new ways to colour code and highlight texts as we began to exchange notes, drafts and comments. Richa Singh's location in the town of Sitapur allowed her the most stable access to email and phone; she became the obvious choice of the group for the person who should serve as a link between the group and me when I was located in the U.S. After preparing each draft, I emailed it as an attachment to Richa Singh, who then circulated it among all the autobiographers for feedback, corrections and suggestions for further revisions. Each chapter went through four to six rounds of feedback and revision in this way.

After all the chapters were drafted in December 2003, the authors came together once again to read them and to identify and address some of the silences that remained. This time, the reflections inspired questions on the process of remembering and writing, on reinterpreting experiences and relationships, as well as the issues of reshaping organizational structures and practices. For example, we wondered why the autobiographers could not remember any happy moments when they wrote their diaries on childhood. We compared notes on how the class, caste and religious locations of each autobiographer shaped the nature of seclusion she experienced in her home and village. We argued over the relationships between *purdah* and oppression, and between absolute and relative poverty, and we debated whether our positions as *sangtins* gave us the right to make judgements about each other's personal choices pertaining to sexuality or religion. The collective pondered over the precise message that it wished to communicate to the readers about the relationships between mothers-in-law and daughters-in-law in rural communities.

With these discussions, the activists also began to imagine, in concrete terms, the challenges that they were likely to face in building structures of transparency in Sangtin. We pushed ourselves to ask what it would mean to decentralize leadership and key responsibilities in Sangtin. We also considered the diverse spectrum of women's organizing in the NGO sector, and decided that Sangtin would have to exist and find resources to grow on the basis of its own internally set priorities, terms and conditions, rather than those imposed by a funding agency. It took three additional rounds of revisions, reading and feedback before these conversations were satisfactorily incorporated into the final version of the manuscript.

Thus, *Sangtin Yatra* was the product of a complex cycle of discussion, writing, reflection, revision and back to discussion. The open but organized format of our collaboration gave us the space and flexibility to grow as a collective as the process unfolded. As we discovered our evolving needs and identified the possibilities created by our collaboration, we reworked our methodology to meet those needs and possibilities.

A Blended but Fractured 'We'

The chorus of nine voices in *Playing with Fire* does not remain constant throughout the book. As one of us speaks, the voice of the second or third suddenly blends in to give an entirely new and unique flavour to our music. Our notes blend, disperse in ones or twos or sevens, and regroup. Below I describe some of the choices that were involved in deciding who would or would not be part of the chorus, and when and how the voices shall sing.

The use of a blended 'we' is a deliberate strategy on the collective's part, as is our decision to share quotes from the diaries in a minimal way. Rather than encouraging our readers to follow the trajectories of the lives of seven women, we braid the stories to highlight our analysis of specific moments in those lives. At the same time, our narrative evolves in the same dialogic manner that our journey did, and in the process, it seeks to open up spaces where the primary intended readers of the original book—other

NGO workers and members of the authors' own communities—can insert their own narratives and reflections in the dialogue. We want to interrupt the popular practice of representation in the media, NGO-reports and academic analyses, where the writing voice of the one who is analysing or reporting as the 'expert' is separated from the voices of the people who are recounting their lives or opinions. One way in which we have chosen to eliminate this separation is by ensuring that our nine voices emerge as a chorus, even if the diaries of only seven of us are the focus of our discussions.

At no time is this unity meant to achieve resolution on issues of casteism, communalism and hierarchy within the collective, however. From the outset, the desire that this journey be about 'opening sealed boxes tucked away in our hearts' (Chapter One) translated into an assumption that issues of power hierarchies could be raised fearlessly only if there were no expectations of resolution. In other words, the 'blended we' hinged on the trust and honesty with which each author could articulate her disagreements and tensions. Bitterness, anger, suspicion and conflict within the collective produced as many tears in the journey as pains and sorrows produced by 'others' did. No meeting of the collective ended without tears at some point. The next six chapters, therefore, frequently bear traces of the wounds and scars that exist within the collective—for example, when we confront questions of relative hunger and deprivation (Chapter Two), untouchability, communalism and casteism (Chapters Two and Four), sexuality (Chapters Two and Three), negotiations over salaries, *purdah* and respectability (Chapter Five) and rank and hierarchy in NGO work (Chapters Four and Six). Yet, as an alliance of transnational actors, we want the readers to be aware that the analysis and stances shared in the book are not merely a collection of individual stories but a result of a collective journey.

But even a fractured unity in voices could not be achieved without first making a tough decision about which language we could speak or write in. The activists' past work had exposed them to the idea that writing and reflection on autobiographical narratives could become useful tools for critical literacy and reflexive activism. However, their desire to undertake such a project also made it necessary for the autobiographers to write in *khadi boli* (Hindi) instead of Awadhi, the language with which they connected more intimately.[17] At the same time, the group's painful awareness of their own location in relation to the elite status of English meant that they always saw writing in Hindi as a political act. Months later, when the collective decided to publish a book in Hindi, this political act assumed greater significance. Authoring our own ideas in Hindi implied that those ideas were being produced, first and foremost, for the group's own communities, friends and close allies, rather than being disseminated to the activists from above. In retrospect, we are also convinced that the impact that *Sangtin Yatra* was able to have was due as much to the nature of our alliance, as to our writing it in Hindi.[18]

The collective's next major challenge emerged in the form of a huge but inevitable contradiction: We sought to reshape the discourse and praxis of empowerment by eliminating hierarchies in Sangtin's organizational structure and future work. In order to achieve this goal, however, we had to confront the reality of unequal distribution of 'skills' within the collective. To begin with, the autobiographers were themselves differentiated—not only by caste, religion, salaries and social status—but also by varying levels of formal education and opportunities they had received as workers in the NGO sector. Second, although they knew that their narratives and work formed the lynchpin of this collaboration, the members of Sangtin also realized from the outset that the process would be difficult to undertake and sustain if Richa Singh and I did not play a prominent role in all phases of the journey: in co-ordinating the discussions; in editing, writing and framing the collective analysis for the book; in strategic decision-making during and after the publishing process; and in assembling the resources necessary for each of these phases to happen. The challenge, then, was to recognize the nature of involvement of both Richas while also asking how the different kinds of skills and resources that each Richa could bring to the journey were a manifestation of the structural inequalities pervasive in the social system in which each of us was embedded; and the role that Sangtin could play in changing that system.

Furthermore, although Richa Singh and I can by no means be described as coming from the 'same background' our Hindu-upper caste affiliations and our socio-economic and geographical locations and histories were radically different from the differences that existed among the autobiographers. Both Richas' diaries on childhood, youth and marriage also side-tracked the discussion towards contexts, issues and power relationships that were not shaped by the politics of NGO work, rural women's empowerment, and knowledge production about rural women's lives in the same ways as the lives of the other seven authors were. The collective decided that Richa Singh and I would write and share our personal stories, but these would become part of the collective's discussions only when they seemed relevant to the issues that the autobiographers' diaries inspired.

Confronting Hierarchy in Alliance: The Politics of 'Skills'

Working out the details of the collaborative process allowed us to interrogate pre-given notions of an 'expert,' and to challenge the dichotomy between 'political' labour (e.g., grassroots activism) and 'intellectual' labour (e.g., sharing of scholarly knowledge, research, writing) even as we continued to (re)work and rely on the skills that each of us had accumulated over the years. For each diary writer, the most important task was to honestly share what she had learned about issues of caste, class and gender from her life and work and to help other members of the collective understand the complexities that she had grappled with, while also making herself vulnerable to critique by the group.

As a co-ordinator of NSY-Sitapur, where the seven diary writers had been employed for varying lengths of time, Richa Singh had provided leadership to this group for six years. She had also been involved in the selection process that introduced each activist to the world of women's NGOs. She was intimately familiar with not only the context and circumstances of the seven autobiographers, but also with their personalities and temperaments, the group dynamics, as well as tensions that existed within the group on issues pertaining to class, caste and religion. These insights, combined with Richa Singh's commitment to the goals of this project, the sensitivity and openness with which she approached each issue, and the respect and trust that she had won from the authors, placed her in a unique position to advance this journey. She not only made sure that we could come together when we wished to, but also made critical interventions that allowed us to draw connections among the stories, to recast our collective memory as we struggled with issues of our own casteism and communalism, and to constructively alter the dynamics within the group by reflecting on its own biases and power struggles. For example, Richa Singh pushed the group to confront the ways in which the Sawarn members of the collective might be participating in the silencing of some voices. At times, she reminded the collective of specific situations that the activists had encountered and sparked discussions on sensitive questions—such as practices of untouchability within the group—that remained otherwise unaddressed in the diaries and conversations. Richa Singh also encouraged the rest of us to openly challenge her own authority and power, and the contradictions buried in her position and engagements with the collective.

At the time we began this journey, the eight activists regarded me as a co-traveller who could play an important role in mapping out with them Sangtin's future directions. By the time we decided to write *Sangtin Yatra*, the tears, laughter, songs and secrets we had shared with each other, had changed our relationship from one between nine co-travellers to one between *sangtins*. Initially, the members of Sangtin were excited about my skills as a Hindi creative writer and a researcher who had worked with NGOs in U.P. They felt that I could play a useful role in helping them address two kinds of constraints that they were under. First, their previous encounters with personal narratives of rural women had been primarily in the form of vignettes where women's experiences of struggle and survival were presented by the more formally educated members of the NGO staff as 'case-studies' or 'achievements' in NGO publications. In addition, their own analytical framework on the politics of gender, caste, communalism and social change had evolved mainly from what they had learned within NSY and women's NGOs in U.P. They wanted me to contextualize for them how other individuals or collectives had deployed personal writing in their own work, and to help them situate the work of NGOs in the wider socio-political terrain of struggles for social change. As village- and district-level NGO workers who had been denied opportunities to analyse how their local struggles were linked to issues at the national and international scales, the group wanted to develop new analytical tools to understand these mutually constitutive processes. Later, with the group's consent, Richa Singh and I undertook the responsibility of leading the writing and publication process in consultation with all the authors.

However, even as my location and privileges made it my responsibility and honour to guide these processes, I could not free myself from anxieties about writing. Although the autobiographers were involved at every stage in the making of *Sangtin Yatra*, they were also convinced that their main job was to write and reflect on their lives and work, and not to learn how to write a book. Whenever I became anxious about how this division of labour gave me the power to represent the collective and this journey, the group tried to allay my concerns by reminding me that forming an alliance was primarily about strategically combining—not replicating—our complementary skills. As Richa Singh and Ramsheela once explained to me:

> We have the skill of doing activism; you have the skill of writing. We do complementary things—that is why we are an alliance. If we taught you how to mobilize women in our villages now, it will take you a few years to get good at it. Similarly, you are teaching us how to write and edit a book, but it will take us a few years to write a good book. Maybe it is not even the best use of our time to write a book! We need to be doing as much work as we can do on the ground, and you need to be writing as much as you can about that work. There is nothing wrong in you undertaking the main labour of making the book. It will still remain our book.

What the group was doing in these discussions, I slowly learned, was deconstructing the idea of the scholar or writer as an 'expert' in this kind of collaboration. By repeatedly reframing the issue of writing (and representation) in terms of labour, my co-authors were not simply saying that their labour of educating and mobilizing people in their communities and of writing, reflection and critiques was at least as important as the labour of transforming everything into formal writing. They were also teaching me that the complexities and politics associated with writing were not significantly different from those involved in their own activism. Moreover, by pointing out that my concerns about writing were understood but not shared by them, they also made me reflect on the extent to which I had internalized the very definitions of 'expert' that I was ostensibly interested in dismantling through collaboration. In the process of collaborating, the activists educated me about things I could never 'learn from the books.' They were teaching me just as much about 'empowerment,' 'development' and NGO work and about the politics of Awadhi, Hindi and English as I was teaching them, if not more. They were making me learn how to enact trust, solidarity, openness and generosity in a collaboration, while also educating me about the importance of emotional labour in alliance making. They were also creating an invaluable opportunity for me to learn how to write and publish a book with them.

In this way, the process of collaboration taught us what it meant to become learners and teachers in the collective. Each of us came to see herself as privileged and handicapped in different ways in the arena of skills. The collaboration became a vehicle for us to understand what each of us could bring to the collective so that all of us could become better educated about the issues we had chosen to struggle for. To put it in Freireian terms, we recognized that a true commitment to the goals of our journey meant that none of us could engage in action or reflection without the action and reflection of others.[19]

Naming, Claiming, Silencing and Authorship

Even as we moved toward preparing the final press copy of *Sangtin Yatra*, difficult questions kept resurfacing: We wondered what the consequences of publishing this book could be for each author, and whether we were ready to face those consequences individually and collectively. There was no doubt in any of our minds that all nine *sangtins* were authors of *Sangtin Yatra*. But we repeatedly asked ourselves if it was equally safe for all of us to publicly display our real names and claim authorship of this work. These questions posed enormous ethical dilemmas. The autobiographers had taken a powerful step by deciding that they wanted to come out as writers of their own stories in Hindi. Writing in Hindi made this a book of, by and for NGO workers and rural people, in their opinion. But it also made them vulnerable to possible responses from their families, from the communities among whom they lived and worked, and from the NGOs they interacted with.

The very personal and powerful memories of silencing, shaming, sexuality, and control over bodies that the authors shared with each other in this journey carried enormous symbolic and emotional meanings for us. These were the stories that each author had 'buried' to protect her familial honour, to avoid her family's embarrassment and shame. But once we started this journey, it was as if everyone was convinced that it is only by saying these things out loud, that we would begin to see new dreams. This conviction kept us going, even in the face of opposition from one autobiographer's spouse. In the end, however, the question boiled down to whether and how the autobiographers wanted to see their stories publicized in the book. Each of them had made herself vulnerable in the collective by exposing her most personal, painful and embarrassing memories with respect to her family, community and intimate relationships. Did it make sense to subsequently make herself similarly vulnerable before her readers, and take the risk of having shame recast on her?

But the collaborative process of sharing—and the price of this sharing that the diary writers had to pay in their homes during the first few months of the journey—had made them fearless. After having 'fought in the homes to write our stories' and after having 'said it all to the people who mattered the most,' audiences such as people in the NGO-sector, their bosses and their readers were no longer a source of fear. Every deliberation on the question: 'Do we really want the stories of seven autobiographers to come out in this form?' resulted in the same answer at the end: 'We have already paid the price by telling it to each other. What can the readers take away now? Let them hear our stories.'

At the same time, we were forced to confront the fact that each autobiographer had taken different forms and degrees of risk in sharing her personal stories in *Sangtin Yatra*. While five of the seven diary writers wanted to claim authorship, two wished to remain anonymous. In the end, the autobiographers decided to appear under their real names on the opening page of the book, but chose pseudonyms for themselves and their villages in the remaining text.

The fear of consequences did not end here. The territory of the family and community was a familiar and largely predictable one, and each autobiographer had handled that front multiple times in the course of her previous work (Chapters Four and Five). But there was an entirely unpredictable territory as well—that of urban intellectuals and the upper rung of NGO officials and actors. Although the collective could have never predicted the intensity of NSY's backlash to which we were subjected after the publication of *Sangtin Yatra*, we were nevertheless aware that we had taken some risks by raising the issues of elitism and casteism in women's NGOs in U.P. But really, how awful could the repercussions be if seven women—after subjecting themselves, their families and communities to intense critical scrutiny on matters of social inequalities and discriminatory practices—also turned their lenses in the direction of women's NGOs where they worked to question the hierarchies and double standards there?

Prior to the book's publication, we could think of only two possible negative repercussions: First, in some circles, people might try to dismiss our critique on the grounds that it reflected only my agenda and not the agenda of the collective. The second and more extreme scenario that we could imagine was that Richa Singh might be reprimanded by higher officials in NSY for playing a central role in facilitating this collective effort, and for fully participating in it. We could not imagine that anyone who read the book would dream of attacking the autobiographers for undertaking this labour, no matter how much they agreed or disagreed with our analysis.

We debated the issue of publication multiple times over a period of three months. Finally, the seven diary writers concluded that having come this far, there could be no turning back. It was time to stop revisiting the question of whether the book should come out or not. The book was ready and all the *sangtins* were eager to appear before the world as its authors. It was important to the group that the effort be recognized as one undertaken by the members of Sangtin for charting the future course of that organization, while also giving each collaborator her due recognition for the labour, energy and time that she had contributed to the collective effort. Accordingly, the collective decided that Sangtin itself would publish the book, and determined how the publication process would be organized and how credit for authorship would be given to each writer.

From NSY's Backlash[20] to *Playing with Fire*

Thus, nine collaborators publicly intervened in the politics of knowledge production with an explicit aim of reclaiming the meanings of empowerment and grassroots politics. The scholarly and literary reviewers and media called *Sangtin Yatra* a 'unique effort' and a 'dialogue' through which 'not only Sitapur but the entire Awadh region' had made an 'extraordinary intervention in feminist thought.'[21] Lal Bahadur Verma argued that the 'freshness of hypothesis and methodology' with which *Sangtin Yatra* fights against social orthodoxies not only highlights the 'value of creative struggle, but it also offers a natural invitation to think, understand and do things in new ways that can enact such creative struggle.'[22] With the one-on-one efforts of the activists themselves, the book began to quickly circulate in the homes of NGO staff and workers, where it sparked both emotional responses and questioning of caste and class hierarchies, and also brought recognition for each of us as an 'author' in her family and community. However, the wide media attention and the critiques of elitism and hierarchy in women's NGOs that we raised also triggered a backlash by NSY, U.P. The intensity of both kinds of responses took the collective by surprise. We found our journey thrown onto a new course barely three weeks after *Sangtin Yatra* was released.

The director of NSY, U.P. launched an attack on the nine authors by condemning us for undertaking this effort. Her two main charges were that we had failed to give credit to NSY, and that Richa Singh and I had engaged in irresponsible writing that failed to verify the 'truth' provided by the grassroots workers.

She argued that the autobiographers had gained all their experiences as employees of the NSY and so they had betrayed NSY by writing about their lives and work as members of Sangtin. She wanted the authors to apologize for this 'mistake' in the media. At the same time, she also held that our analysis undermined the efforts of women's organizations.

Every member of the collective refused to issue an apology to the media, denying that we had betrayed NSY, and stating that we had simply exercised our freedom of expression. This led the director to issue charge sheets that threatened to take disciplinary action against the seven authors who were NSY-employees unless they 'showed cause' why the allegations that were placed on them were false, and proved their innocence. The director also urged the chair of my department to take disciplinary action against me. Her most extreme move was to transfer Richa Singh out of Sitapur district despite opposition from women of Mishrikh block and workers of NSY-Sitapur who pleaded to stop the transfer. The transfer order resulted in a struggle for seven months to get the order withdrawn and climaxed in Richa Singh's protest resignation from NSY.

We were struck by the way in which this furious response reinforced the very critiques that we had raised in the book, while taking a form that we had not imagined. The collective's struggle to fight this attack on the livelihoods, integrity and basic human and constitutional rights of the authors was all consuming, especially as we were, once again, scattered in two continents. The authors began by responding to the accusations verbally in formal meetings and through writing letters. We also felt an urgent need to make the contents of our book available to readers outside the Hindi-speaking world so that we could reach out for their support if necessary; and I started translating *Sangtin Yatra* into English. But the backlash was fierce and when it continued to intensify over a period of eight weeks, the collective decided to reach out to friends and supporters with an email petition to stop the attacks on the authors of *Sangtin Yatra*.

Petitioning, organizing and strategizing across eight villages, two districts and two oceans was not easy—logistically, economically or emotionally. But we were energized by the overwhelming positive support we received from progressive intellectuals and activists, in and outside India. The attack on the book, furthermore, made each author more confident than ever that we had done the right thing and that our collaboration was sparking a response in the very circles we wanted to reach. It is also noteworthy that the autobiographers' families rose in support of *Sangtin Yatra*. When one prominent 'feminist' NGO trainer accused the collective of stripping the autobiographers naked before the public, we were pained by the deep contradiction buried in her accusation. We asked why the autobiographers had always been encouraged to interrogate patriarchy by revealing their personal stories and intimate experiences in organizational meetings, and why the same stories amounted to 'stripping oneself naked' when they chose to break the silences on the politics of NGO work. When these discussions reached the homes of the authors, it was the so-called patriarchal husbands and families of the autobiographers who declared: 'Don't even think of apologizing or explaining anything to your employers. If they make more accusations, we will answer them.'

It was this kind of broad public support gained by *Sangtin Yatra* that led Richa Singh to resign from NSY with an open protest against the actions of the Director of NSY, U.P. and how they mocked the very idea of empowerment. In her official notice of resignation, Richa Singh wrote:

> After the publication of *Sangtin Yatra* by Sangtin, you subjected me to a punitive action by transferring me out of Sitapur . . . *Sangtin Yatra* seeks to advance feminist thought, but you labeled our collective writing as a gruesome criminal act . . ., and repeatedly tortured me for supporting this work . . . .[Your] decisions . . . have clearly shown me how even in a programme such as [NSY] that works to empower women, a worker can be subjected to social, economic and mental torture if her voice is different from the voice of the higher officials . .
>
> This is not empowerment, but a vulgar joke in the name of rural women's empowerment . . . . [It was in NSY] where I learned to fight for my rights and entitlements, and where I was given the role of teaching others how to fight the same battle; in that same [NSY], I . .
>
> cannot live in this relationship of servitude. In opposition . . . to the decisions you have taken in regard to *Sangtin Yatra*, I submit this notice [of resignation].[23]

Despite the strain and difficulties posed by it, NSY's backlash has been helpful for our future work. We never expected *Sangtin Yatra* to get so much support immediately after publication. In addition, our transnational strategizing to counter the backlash has helped us to strengthen as well as broaden our alliance and pushed us considerably further in our thinking than we had expected in such a short time. Yet, as we fought against Richa Singh's transfer and worried about the survival of the energy that *Sangtin Yatra* had created, we reminded ourselves that our long-term challenge is to ensure that Sangtin can continue translating its dreams into reality without making compromises it does not wish to make. But in order to realize this dream, it is also critical that we continue our struggle to build and multiply the spaces for more *yatras* in which more *sangtins* can come together to reclaim the meanings of empowerment, and to intervene in the global politics of knowledge production from their own locations, perspectives and priorities.

And this is our reason for playing with fire for the third time. The publication of *Sangtin Yatra* was to gain recognition for the *sangtins*' analysis and critiques in places where the activists were located. The English translation of *Sangtin Yatra* was initially undertaken (and circulated) to gain allies to fight NSY's backlash. With the transformation of *Sangtin Yatra* into *Playing with Fire*, the latter's simultaneous publication in New Delhi by Zubaan and in Minneapolis by the University of Minnesota Press, as well as the translations of *Sangtin Yatra* into other Indian languages, we continue our struggle to create more spaces and legitimacy for journeys such as this. We have come to see this journey as an alliance across the borders of Awadhi, Hindi and English—an alliance that allows us to show how each member of this collective is not only inserted in transnational systems of knowledge production, but that her own life and political and intellectual engagements are deeply impacted by such production. In seeking recognition for the intellectual worth of our journey, we argue for a need for greater accountability in knowledge production—whether that knowledge is produced by researchers, reporters, NGO workers, academic institutions or think tanks. Such a notion of accountability is based on the idea that knowledges must emerge out of sustained, critical dialogues with those who are the subjects of that knowledge. Through these dialogues, the subjects of knowledge become the primary evaluators, critics and intellectual partners of those who are seen as the 'experts.' Thus, discourses such as 'empowerment,' 'critical pedagogy' and 'feminist praxis' get enhanced and enriched as they are collaboratively theorized, used, critiqued, revised and reshaped to gain new forms of relevance and resonance across borders.

Embracing this goal comes with myriad risks, of course. There is the danger of a renewed attack by NSY officials against the livelihoods of the six authors who are still employed there and who have been often denigrated in the aftermath of *Sangtin Yatra*. There is a risk that the anger that Sangtin is already facing from certain quarters of the NGO sector would intensify with the publication of *Playing with Fire*. There is the vexed question of the kind of inequalities this version of *Sangtin Yatra* might create in a collective where I am the only author who can participate fluently in international discussions of the translated parts of this journey. And there is also the ever present threat—one that we have encountered in the media representations as well as in NSY's past attacks—of our alliance being misinterpreted or portrayed as an instrumentalist and exploitative strategy to establish Sangtin or one or more of its authors. Aware of these risks, the *sangtins* have decided to play with fire for two simple reasons. First, it would be yet another test of the durability of our alliance. Second, without *Playing with Fire*, we will never know how long or far this journey or similar other journeys can go, or what they can ultimately achieve.

Notes

[1] One of the eight authors, Surbala, left her job at NSY in 2000, while Richa Singh resigned in 2004.

[2] In terms of our religious and caste affiliations, six of us can be labeled as Sawarn Hindu; two as Dalit; and one as Sunni Muslim. These affiliations broadly parallel those that exist in the Sawarn Hindu-dominated NGO sector active in Sitapur district. Also, three things (not obvious from my institutional affiliation) that allowed me to become a part of this alliance were my close association with U.P., my home state

where my family lives and where I have worked with NGO workers since 1996; my thirst for writing in Hindi/Hindustani; and my close familiarity with Awadhi.

[3] Awadhi, or the language of Awadh, is predominantly spoken in the rural areas of central and eastern U.P., including the districts of Bahraich, Barabanki, Faizabad, Gonda, Hardoi, Lakheempur, Lucknow, Raibareli, Sitapur, Sultanpur and Unnao. Although some written literature in Awadhi exists, for the most part Awadhi remains a spoken language. For those who grow up with Awadhi as their native tongue, then, the process of becoming 'literate' in their 'own' language often implies becoming literate in Hindi or *khadi boli* (see Glossary).

[4] The authors' collective met in December 2004 to discuss the possibility of publishing *Sangtin Yatra*'s second edition in Hindi. Revisions and updating of the original *Sangtin Yatra* for greater clarity of intended meaning were first done collectively in Hindi and then incorporated into *Playing with Fire*. The drafts of Introduction, Postscript and Glossary of *Playing with Fire* were discussed in entirety and revised with all the authors of the collective.

[5] The term 'Hindustani' resists the often artificially imposed compartmentalization between spoken Hindi and Urdu.

[6]Empowerment has become a buzzword whose definitions and uses vary widely. Because 'empowerment' is both a goal of Sangtin as well as a focus of the authors' critique in *Playing with Fire*, it is important to explain the sense in which Sangtin views empowerment. Sangtin's vision of empowerment, fleshed out in Chapter Six, can be seen as paralleling the definition provided by Bina Agarwal in 'Gender and Command Over Property: A Critical Gap in Economic Analysis and Policy in South Asia,' (*World Development* 22:10 (1994): 1455-1478). Agarwal sees empowerment as 'a process that enhances the ability of disadvantaged ("powerless") individuals or groups to challenge and change (in their favour) existing power relationships that place them in subordinate economic, social and political positions.' At the same time, *Sangtin Yatra* has also inspired a vision that aims to empower the local communities intellectually by interrogating the very concept of 'marginality' in a Freireian vein. See Paulo Freire's *Pedagogy of the Oppressed* (New York: The Continuum Publishing Company, 1993). Freire (55) points out that 'the oppressed are not "marginals," are not people living "outside" society. They have always been "inside"—inside the structure which made them "beings for others." The solution is not to "integrate" them into the structure of oppression, but to transform that structure so that they can become "beings for themselves."'

[7] In the six chapters that form this book's second part, *A Journey of Sangtins*, 'we' refers mainly (but not always) to the seven autobiographers. Sometimes, when the authors speak as members of Sangtin or as

community-based workers who have grown together in the context of their activist work, Richa Singh is very much part of the 'we.' And sometimes, when the nine authors write about their process of learning and growing together as a collective, the 'we' includes Richa Singh and Richa Nagar.

[8] Gillian Rose, 'Situating Knowledge: Positionality, Reflexivities and Other Tactics,' *Progress in Human Geography* 21:3 (1997): 305-320; Richa Nagar, 'Footloose Researchers, Traveling Theories and the Politics of Transnational Feminist Praxis,' *Gender, Place and Culture* 9:2 (2002): 179-186.

[9] 'NGOization' is being increasingly recognized as a world-wide phenomenon both in academic work, and in public, intellectual and community spaces of U.P., where this project emerged. In all cases, the usage of this term often involves an implicit or explicit critique that NGOs and their ties with the state are significantly reshaping, even replacing, community-based activism. See, for example, Arundhati Roy, 'Tide? Or Ivory Snow? Public Power in the Age of Empire,' Speech given in San Francisco, California on August 16, 2004. Roy calls this phenomenon 'The NGO-ization of politics [that] threatens to turn resistance into a well-mannered, reasonable, salaried, 9-to-5 job. With a few perks thrown in.' Downloaded August 18 from: http://www.democracynow.org/static/Arundhati_Trans.shtml

NGOization is by no means confined to the 'third world.' For example, Sabine Lang, 'The NGO-ization of Feminism: Institutionalization and Institution Building Within the German Women's Movement;' in *Global Feminisms Since 1945*, ed. Bonnie Smith (New York: Routledge, 2002), 291-292, notes in the context of Germany:

> German women's movements have metamorphosed from overarching movements into small scale professionalized organizations. ... The transition from movement to NGO brought with it a structural emphasis on professionalized but decentralized small-scale organizations and a turn from anti-hierarchical to more hierarchical structures. Ideologically, there is a tendency to translate the "traditionally" complex feminist agenda of emancipation and equality into specific single issues and a form of politics with a predominantly state-oriented focus. While feminist movement building was once about the establishment of new democratic counterculture, feminist organizations today are about issue-specific intervention and pragmatic strategies that have a strong employment focus.

[10] See Sangeeta Kamat, *Development Hegemony: NGOs and the State in India* (New Delhi: Oxford University Press, 2002); Marnia Lazreg, 'Development: Feminist Theory's Cul-de-sac,' in *Feminist Postdevelopment Thought: Rethinking Modernity, Postcolonialism, Representation*, ed. Kriemild Saunders (London: Zed Press, 2002); Vijay

Pratap, 'Some Reflections on Funding and Volunteerism,' *Lokayan Bulletin* 12: 3 (1995): 1-4; Chachage Seithy L. Chachage, 'The World Social Forum: Lessons from Mumbai,' *The African* (daily, Dar es Salaam, Tanzania) appeared in six installments Feb 23-28; Roy, 'Tide? Or Ivory Snow?'

[11] The demographic statistics on Sitapur are based on the 2001 Census of India, downloaded from http://www.censusindia.net/t_00_003.html on January 29, 2005 and from http://sitapur.nic.in/ on October 8, 2004. Other information about socio-political context of Sitapur provided in this section comes from the informal surveys done by members of the authors' collective in relation to their *field*-activities and volunteer work.

[12] Bibek Debroy and Laveesh Bhandari, eds., *District-level Deprivation in the New Millennium* (New Delhi: Konark Publishers Pvt Ltd, 2003). The identification of these 'most backward' districts is based on estimated poverty ratios, percentage of households going hungry, infant mortality rates, levels of immunization, literacy rates and enrollment ratios for 2001. Women's social status is reflected in Sitapur's low sex ratio, which has increased in the last decade from 833 to 862 females per thousand males.

[13] For historical overviews and critical analyses of women's movements in colonial and postcolonial India, see Radha Kumar, *The History of Doing: An illustrated account of movements for women's rights and feminism in India*, 1800-1990 (New Delhi: Kali for Women, 1993); Samita Sen, 'Towards a Feminist Politics? The Indian Women's Movement in Historical Perspective,' in *The Violence of Development: The Politics of Identity, Gender and Social Inequalities in India*, ed. Karin Kapadia (New Delhi: Kali for Women, 2002) 459-524; Mary E. John, 'Feminism, Poverty and Globalization: An Indian View,' *Inter-Asia Cultural Studies*, 3:3 (2002): 351-367.

[14] Such encouragement by NSY for village-level workers to form their own organization seems to be undergoing reconsideration in the aftermath of the controversy surrounding *Sangtin Yatra*.

[15] See note # 4.

[16] The group's interest in South Africa was sparked by a recent visit to Sitapur by a group of 40 South African experts affiliated with NGOs, who had been sent there by the state office of NSY,.U.P.

[17] See note # 3.

[18] I return to this point in the Postscript.

[19] Friere, *Pedagogy of the Oppressed*, 107.

[20] Further details about the backlash are discussed in the Postscript.

[21] Shikha Srivastava, 'Likhna, Aurat Ki Zindagi!' *Hindustan, Adaab Lucknow* [Hindi daily, Lucknow] April 1, 2004, 1; Maitreyi Pushpa, 'Baden Laanghti Striyan,' *Rashtriya Sahara* [Hindi daily, New Delhi], March 20, 2004, 9; Bandhu Kushawarti, 'Saat Zindagiyon Mein Lipta Nari Vimarsh,' *Aakhir Kab Tak?* [Hindi periodical, Lucknow] 2:6 (2004): 26; Newsreport,

Amar Ujala [Hindi daily, Kanpur] March 26, 2004, 6; Pratibha Katiyar, 'Sangtin Yatra: Pustak Vimochan,' *Uttar Pradesh* [Hindi monthly, Lucknow] May 2004, 31-32.

All translations from Hindi into English in *Playing with Fire* are by Richa Nagar

[22] Translated from Hindi. Lal Bahadur Verma, 'Tootte Pinjare—Naye Asman,' *Vagarth* [Hindi monthly, Kolkata] Nov, 2004, 26. Verma is a retired Professor of History from the University of Allahabad and edits the history journal, *Itihaas Bodh*.

[23] Richa Singh's official notice to the Director of NSY, U.P., Oct 1, 2004.

Part II

A Journey of Sangtins

Sangtin Writers

Anupamlata, Ramsheela, Reshma Ansari, Richa Nagar
Richa Singh, Shashibala, Shashi Vaish, Surbala,
Vibha Bajpayee

The Beginnings of A Collective Journey

Seven women, seven lives, countless aspirations, worlds, dreams and struggles. Sometimes, the threads of our lives get entangled with each other, and at others, they isolate themselves and scatter. Sometimes, they grab us so tightly that it is impossible for us to contain waves of tears, and at others we cannot begin to fathom how breathing in the same world, our pauses, our turns and our encounters could be so different from each others'.[1] There are so many gulfs we had not experienced...so many wounds we had not known... The walls, absences and oppressions that defined the daily lives of some of us seemed quite remote to the rest—not only in terms of our ability to imagine the pain they cause, but also the courage and creativity that it takes to live and enjoy life amidst these. This collective journey has changed that reality forever...

"A journey of our lives and work"—this is how we named this effort and this contract, into which we decided to enter in December 2002. The stories, the joys and sorrows, the struggles and dreams that we are about to share with you mark the first halt in this journey. What we have achieved in this first phase of our journey is difficult to describe—a self-confidence, a collective spirit, a deep respect for each other, and a much sharper vision to live and fight in a society whose chains burn us with rage and ignite us to smash and break them. At the same time, it is only by suffering under the weight of those chains that we are able to imagine new possibilities that allow us to chart the directions of our upcoming battles.

Before we talk about our struggles and stories, it is important that we begin with our process and objectives: Who are we? How did we come together and decide to enter into this collective contract? How did we determine our process? How did we weave our nine voices? And how did we accomplish the work of writing this book despite the enormous distances, hardships and inequalities that divided us?

The stories and analyses that we are about to share with you in this journey of *sangtins* are based on discussions of personal diaries of seven grassroots workers. These women are affiliated with a small voluntary organization called Sangtin in the Mishrikh block of Sitapur district in Uttar Pradesh. They initially came together as a result of their work as village-level mobilizers in NSY, a well-known women's organization that works in the rural areas of Uttar Pradesh. Over the years, all seven women have gained visibility and recognition as local grassroots workers. The names with which the diary writers emerge as characters of their own lives in the pages of this book are Chaandni, Garima, Madhulika, Pallavi, Radha, Sandhya and Shikha.

To share, blend and weave their experiences and struggles, these seven diary writers built an alliance with each other and with Richa Singh and Richa Nagar.

Richa Singh first joined NSY in 1991 as an office assistant. By 1996, she established herself as an able leader and arrived in Sitapur to co-ordinate NSY's newly launched programme in Sitapur district. In 1998, she co-founded Sangtin with eight co-workers from NSY so that the work of mobilizing rural women may continue after the completion of the time-bound programme of NSY.

Richa Nagar has been acquainted with members of Sangtin since 1996. In 1989, Richa Nagar went from Lucknow to Minneapolis to seek a Ph.D. in geography from the University of Minnesota (USA). She now teaches there in the Department of Women's Studies.

Richa Singh and Richa Nagar became familiar with each other through the activities of various women's organizations in Uttar

Pradesh. In June 1996, Richa Nagar had an opportunity to spend a few days participating in and learning about the work that Richa Singh was doing in Sitapur. After that meeting, the two Richas did not get a chance to interact closely until March 2002, when Richa Singh suddenly dropped in one day to see Richa Nagar in Lucknow. From there began a series of meetings, conversations and relationships. Today, we take a pause to translate the first phase of our journey into this book. Our wish is to reach people working at all levels in the NGO sector, and with them, we want the children and school teachers in our villages to read this book. And most of all, we want village-level NGO workers to read the story of our collective journey, so that the process of exchanging stories and sharing courage that we have begun here may carry on.

Politics of Knowledge Production and the Emergence of a Collective Methodology

The eight members of Sangtin who became a part of this collaboration may not have known from the beginning that we were going to become writers, but living in the middle of voluntary organizations, we had become fully aware that the processes of assembling, serving, distributing and consuming knowledge on any subject are always political. Often, we feel that while working collectively in the *field* we are able to identify and resolve complex issues with sensitivity. But in places where we are dominated by an elite English speaking crowd, we hesitate to talk about our own accomplishments. Individuals who are far less informed than us about the issues and communities we work among, sometimes seize credit for our work on the strength of English and sometimes we are forced to accept their interpretations of our work that we disagree with. Similarly, we are expected to stretch and resize the nature and significance of our work when we have to present it before funding agencies or important personalities. In these scenarios, we are forced to say what they wish to hear.

We wondered why those who live and do the most challenging work with Dalit and the poorest communities are rarely the ones who get invited to participate in conversations about that work, or to prepare reports, articles and books on it. When feminist thought is discussed in various fora, we asked, why are some people considered worthy of presenting their viewpoints and some are invited simply for exhibition? We had realized that these issues are related to various inequalities residing in our society. But it was only at the personal level that we had recognized these facts as painful realities; we had not had a chance to discuss these issues or develop a perspective about them in a systematic manner.

Between 1997 and 1999, our work in NSY received a lot of attention inside and outside Uttar Pradesh when the women in the villages of Mishrikh took on the festival of *Gudiya* and the practices associated with the post-wedding custom of *Shagun* and launched a powerful attack on anti-woman values and traditions. As soon as the work came into the limelight, researchers started appearing from several places. Someone wished to prepare a research report, whereas another wanted to make a documentary film so that the publicity could help others to learn from our work. Similarly, there were discussions for the need to systematically document and present other work that was being done in Sitapur.

But in Sitapur, women who were involved in this work asked themselves: If we ourselves cannot become a key part of any research or documentation process; if such a process does not aim to advance our own skills and analyses; and if a team of English-educated urban women draped in starched cotton saris uses our work and experiences to conduct a study in intellectual isolation from us, would that work carry any other significant meaning for us besides exploitation?

Not surprisingly, then, when the two Richas first met in March 2002, the primary theme that emerged in their discussion was centred on the politics of research and documentation. Richa Nagar's previous efforts to understand the growing hierarchies and changing structures of accountability in women's NGOs in Uttar Pradesh revealed to her the limits of traditional academic critiques of the politics of NGO work. She was in search of a group of grassroots activists with whom she could build a long-term partnership—a partnership that could foster a multi-dimensional conversation on the inequalities associated with research and documentation processes, and promote an exchange of ideas and skills through which all the collaborators could advance their understandings and struggles, individually and as a collective.

Richa Singh was saddened by the politics of documentation. Women's NGOs were being increasingly pressured by funding agencies, which attached no value to grassroots work until that work was measured by the standards of the funders and packaged into glossy, computerized reports full of statistics. The NGO workers in the villages—who worked tirelessly without regard to the hour of the day, or the credit received in the form of accolades or money, and who repeatedly rebelled and made compromises in their personal lives to immerse themselves in a social struggle against inequalities based on caste, class and gender, were not consulted about how much depth there was in the reports and figures that claimed to measure empowerment. No one bothered to find out the extent to which this kind of reporting met with their consent or satisfaction. And no one informed them about the reasons for which they were being forced to produce specific kinds of reports about their work.

When seven more members of Sangtin joined Richa Singh and Richa Nagar to delve into these and similar issues, new questions and hopes began to emerge. Together, we began to ask: Who gets to represent the work of a specific class of activists in feminist thought, and why? How are these processes linked with the changing nature of women's organizations? Is it not possible that the village-level workers themselves could write about and account for their *own* work on rituals and traditions, violence and casteism? Could the nine of us join hands and brains in such a way that the work of activists on the ground, and the labour of reading, writing, analysing and theorizing about that work could be interwoven like the threads of a backstitch? Could we shape a collaboration that refused to be reduced to a project, report or case study done for someone else, but that could advance our own skills and abilities, and energize us to weave our dreams for the future on the basis of our own priorities rather than the agendas of a funding agency?

The spark generated by this conversation in March 2002 did not die with Richa Nagar's departure to the U.S. On the contrary, it intensified on all sides—through letters and group discussions.

After careful reflection, we decided to undertake this work collectively. But how should we concretely outline this collaboration? How many people should participate in it and who should they be? What should be the basis of including some and excluding others? All these issues remained undetermined until December 2002, when Richa Nagar returned to Sitapur. After a series of conversations with eighty women, it was decided that in the first phase of this collaboration there should be eight to ten members of Sangtin who have worked for the longest period with rural women in Sitapur. As actors forming the link between Sangtin and the villages, these members are closely familiar with the issues and backgrounds of rural women as well as with the politics of NGO work, and they are also able to express themselves in written *khadi boli*. In the latter half of December, the nine of us gathered to argue, discuss and determine the nature, form, objectives, methods and rules of our collaborative project. The mutual understanding and trust emerging from these in-depth discussions gave our collaboration a force that enabled us to collectively determine every aspect of this project—from the big and small expenses to each word that appears in this book.

There are two noteworthy things about the detailed programme of work that we sketched out in these discussions. First, we were fully aware while outlining our project that the methodology of any long-term project is never stable. As the work advances it often becomes necessary to modify several of its aspects. Second, we did not make a firm decision that we will give a specific form to the product(s) of our collaboration, or that we will even share it publicly with people outside Sangtin. Our main goal at the outset was to imagine and mould a methodology that would enable us to reflect and understand our lives and work, and give us the strength and perspective to envision our future direction. We recognized that there would be moments in this journey that we would have anticipated, and others about which we would not have the slightest clue in advance. The writing of this book is also such a moment—we mentioned it as a possibility in our group conversations in December 2002, but none of us had really imagined that eight months later, we would be selecting excerpts from our diaries and conversations to envision the various chapters of this book.

From Ink to Tears: A Long Partnership

When we first collected our thoughts to begin writing our diaries, the first question that arose was: We have never written a diary before! How will we write this, then? What will we write and what will we leave unwritten? Are we obliged to share every word that we write, or can certain pieces remain unshared? Rather than having a discussion on these questions, we started exploring our answers with the help of diary writing itself. In the lukewarm sun of December, some of us sat on the same *chatai* as we drowned ourselves in our lives; while others scattered under the trees and in the spaces of roofs and corridors. We all wrote for an hour—primarily on our childhoods. When we returned to the circle to share our writing with the group, and started reading our words one after another, it was impossible to contain the monsoon clouds that started flowing from nine pairs of eyes.

We knew in that instant that this work of writing and sharing would be beautiful. But where would we find the time to write? How will we find a corner, a place, where we can sit and fearlessly write on the pages of our diaries all those tears that have been welling up inside us for years and never stopped hurting?

Once the words started pouring from our pens and hearts, it was impossible to check their flow. And before we could make any rule about what could or could not be shared, Chaandni shook all of us. The story of her painful separation from her first daughter—a story she had hidden in a tiny box in her heart for seventeen years and about which she had sealed her lips because she had vowed before her father and husband not to repeat it to anyone—suddenly that story poured out of her lips like a poet reads her most painful and loved poem. Chaandni, who was the last one to join our group, trusted the group and shared this secret without any hesitation, as if she were saying to the group: "Now, this burden is not simply mine. You have all become my partners in it." The trust that she instantly placed in this group and in our collective process by opening the sealed box tucked away in her heart moved us so much that her act came to symbolize the biggest objective of our journey: trust and transparency in collective reflection. After this, it was clear that we would share everything that we wrote; otherwise, our goal of advancing our understanding through collective writing would remain incomplete.

And the group remained loyal to this partnership. For example, in the bitter cold of January 2003, even as Madhulika was reaching the end of her pregnancy, the group met overnight to discuss what we had written about our childhoods. Soon after the discussion, Madhulika started having labour pains and with the assistance of all the companions, Chaandni delivered Madhulika's son at 3:30 AM. This was a very auspicious, happy and meaningful beginning to our journey as writers.

Another episode that connected our hearts occurred within a few weeks, when Chaandni's husband read the section of her diary where she had written in detail about her youth and sexuality. He was enraged. Threatening to kill himself, he walked out of the house. Radha, who lived in the same village, went with her own husband to calm him down and brought Chaandni's husband back home. However, when Radha returned to her own home, her husband insisted on reading certain portions of her personal writing and Radha had to share them with him.

It is not possible to describe in words how some of us wrote these invaluable documents in secrecy...in the dim light of tiny kerosene lamps...as we hid ourselves in the quilts amidst our husbands and children at night... and the number of personal risks and dangers that we embraced in order to write these diaries. Every time Sandhya touched her diary she thought about that deliberately erased night from her infancy when her father was killed in a riot. Radha relived every moment of those insults and injuries that she and her family had to suffer because of being the only Dalit family in their village. Garima and Pallavi bravely shared everything about sexuality and sexual abuse that women with children have to forcibly swallow in the name of respectability, honour and social prestige.

With all this, the group continued to find the tools to give courage to each other—to reflect, remember, write and share. Between January and June 2003, every twenty to twenty-five days the eight members of Sangtin made it a point to complete all their jobs and responsibilities and come together to share what we wrote. No one noticed when the afternoon turned into night and when the next morning crept in. In these meetings, all of us asked each writer every question that we could think of, and entered into the folds of each issue to understand its intricate layers. After so many years of working together, we had all assumed that we knew everything there was to know about each person. But when we started writing the diaries, we felt that we had seen such a small piece of the histories and struggles of our companions. There was so much that remained to be learned within this very group—let alone from the rest of the world. In our conversations, we tried to highlight and confront all the disagreements courageously so that we were not forced to swallow the things that troubled us in the way that our society had forced us to swallow them previously. For example, someone would frequently raise the question that no matter how sensitive a Brahmin woman is to the question of caste difference, can she feel the pain of humiliation and untouchability in the same way as the daughter of a Paasi or Raidas can? Is there not a huge difference between feeling the social violence affecting a specific group from a distance, and in enduring it yourself? Similarly, there were arguments about marriage, sexual attraction and extra-marital relationships.

Later, social status and hierarchy in relation to NGO work also emerged as complicated terrains. We found it problematic that even as we talk about women's rights and collective empowerment in the villages, the organizations working for the same women are being led and guided by individual personalities. Questions of position and status frequently ended up centering on Richa Singh: Why does Richa Singh have a special place in an organization such as NSY? What kinds of contradictions are buried in the title of *Didi*, which people so lovingly call her? Even as we struggled with these issues, however, we recognized the ways in which Richa Singh's leadership and co-ordination have been so critical for our activist work, and how deep and multi-dimensional our relationships are. We were also able to recognize more intimately how as an office assistant and a single mother Richa Singh took on the responsibility of running NSY in Sitapur. No matter how difficult the topic of discussion, we spoke with openness and without softening up the hard edges—even if resolving those issues took a lot of arguments and discomfort later on.

At times, the events in this journey left us shaken for weeks. Tears choked us as we wrote our diaries. All these years we had become so used to hearing about other women's sufferings and joys that we had forgotten to give words to our own stories... to the fading memories of our own childhood and youth, the sufferings of our mothers, our dreams and pains... And amidst these realizations we were also struck by the hollowness of our past discussions on caste and class. We had not identified the extent to which our own relationships and understandings of each other were wrapped in the differences and inequalities of these very same structures.

Perhaps it was after telling and sharing so much that we decided in August 2003, to bring this work out as a book. The thinking behind making this work public was based on the understanding that whenever we reflect deeply and collectively on a set of personal or structural issues, then that reflection ceases to be a critique of a specific individual or organization. It becomes connected to all those social, economic and political conditions and processes within which we are living...Then why should we be afraid of saying everything that happened to us but that we could not speak because our mouths were shut by the tightly pressed hands—belonging sometimes to our mothers and aunts, sometimes to our grandfathers and brothers, sometimes to the people from our *sasural*, and sometimes to our own friends, co-workers, bosses and ministers.

Here it is also necessary for us to say why during the course of this project, both Richas shared their stories with the group, but these did not become a part of the formal diary writing in the same ways as the writing of the rest of the group. When, in December 2002, we were determining the nature and form of this collective writing, we decided that it was appropriate only for those members of the group who had spent the majority of their lives in the rural areas of Sitapur to participate in the formal diary writing. Because Sangtin works in Sitapur and the goal of this journey was to imagine Sangtin's future directions, we felt that this journey should be centred on the experiences of those of us who had emerged as activists in this context, and who had spent most of our time organizing women in the villages of Sitapur.

We also realized that no matter how sensitive we tried to be towards social inequalities, the involvement of the two Richas in formal diary writing would create the danger of sharpening the socio-economic gulfs that existed within our group with respect to educational status, social position and environments. We did not wish for the narratives of Richa Singh and Richa Nagar to dominate the discussions in a way that dimmed our primary focus of learning about the struggles of rural women in the context of the interwoven politics of NGO work, women's empowerment and knowledge production. When the idea of writing a book based on the diaries and discussions came up eight months into the process, the collective revisited these points and concluded that the responsibility of both Richas should be focused on organizing and co-ordinating the discussions in each phase of the book's evolution, and on drafting and revising each chapter until it met with the satisfaction of the collective.

The Mazes of Forgetting and Remembering...

When we collectively began to weave our diaries together, we discovered that the meanings of remembering and forgetting could be quite different for each of us. Which moments are etched forever in our hearts and minds, and which moments refuse to remain in our memories? Why does childhood refuse to become a part of our memory at times, and at others, a single incident weighs so heavily on our hearts that it is impossible to recover and move away from it?

The complexities of these processes can neither be captured by a formula, nor can this kind of writing ever be contained within rules. For this reason, in the following pages you will find that even when a conversation on a specific topic begins, its focus moves in multiple directions. Whereas any mention of childhood brings back memories of hunger and humiliation for Radha, Garima recalls her father's alcoholism and Pallavi is reminded of the sexual abuse she suffered as a little girl. Whenever Chaandni tries to focus on her past, the lenses of her memory fix over and over again on her first marriage, which after subjecting her to many insults and bodily injuries, forced her to separate from her first offspring. Sandhya turns her face away every time the issue of sexuality arises. Her soul trembles at the memory of the murder that caused her family to change her name from Abha (splendour) to Sandhya (evening). Shikha's writing is repeatedly marked by the painful complaint of why she had to endure poverty and hardships throughout her life despite being born in a well-to-do family. And Madhulika is surrounded by the sounds of her own laughter—laughter that her family and relatives hated so much. Whenever Raidas are mentioned in any conversation, Madhulika is filled with a rage and bitterness and wants to bury everyone's voice in silence...

But despite these unstable centres and lenses, every experience and memory remains rooted in its own context, in the politics of social positions and status, honour and dishonour...and in an insuppressible desire to envision and find the courage to fulfil dreams for the future.

We have organized this *Journey of Sangtins* in the same order in which the autobiographers wrote their diaries—first childhood, then youth, marriage and motherhood, and finally the struggles and experiences related to work. It is important that these chapters be read not merely as stories of seven women of Sitapur, but as a way to immerse oneself in the perspectives, visions and thought of nine *sangtins*. For this reason, our last chapter centres on the complexities and politics of contemporary women's organizations. How far can a committed alliance help us in addressing questions pertaining to women's movement and empowerment that are resurfacing in many places today? How have the authors in this collective perceived and evaluated rural women's struggles and the politics of NGO work? Based on an analysis of their own lives and struggles as women and workers, how is this small group charting the course and weaving the dreams for its future? Too often, we hear the answers to these questions from people sitting at the top, but hardly ever from workers operating at the very bottom. This book is an effort to advance these conversations in a new way. With these introductory remarks, then, we begin the story of a collective journey...

Notes

[1] As mentioned in note # 7 of the "Introduction," in the six chapters of *A Journey of Sangtin* (Part II of *Playing with Fire*), "we" refers mainly (but not always) to the seven autobiographers. Sometimes, when the authors speak as members of Sangtin or as community-based workers who have grown together in the context of their activist work, Richa Singh is very much part of the "we." And sometimes, when the nine authors write about the process of learning and growing together as a collective, the "we" includes Richa Singh and Richa Nagar.

A Very Short Childhood

> People often say that you shouldn't teach your children to steal. When I was a child, I told so many lies...stole so many times. Yet, I never formed the habit of stealing. Now I feel that a lie that is told for the good of others is not a lie—it is bigger than the truth.
>
> — From Garima's diary

Since we became associated with women's NGOs, we cannot recount the number of times when we have asked other women to share their personal stories with us, and all the workshops in which we have narrated our own anecdotes and experiences before them. But when we began writing our own stories, we suddenly realized that no one had ever asked us about our childhood! A lifetime seems to have passed since we revisited our lives as children. When we sat down to recollect that forgotten past, such a flood of tears inundated us that we couldn't begin to understand how when other authors think about their past they remember a childhood as colourful as the butterflies, or a past akin to the flight of beautiful birds in faraway skies... Whenever we sat down to write and tell, we just remembered how short that period of our lives was which people label as "childhood." And that childhood, too, was ridden with so many complications and so much suffering, that its memories sometimes reek of casteism and sometimes of alcoholism... sometimes the memories fill up with the pain of being born as a third daughter, and sometimes they are filled with terrorized screams of familial and property-based rivalries...

In the flashbacks that struck our minds, the images we saw were the same familiar ones—of deprivation and poverty, of mothers being beaten mercilessly, and of the wounds and injuries that our own bodies received from the beatings of our parents. Hardly ever could we recall moments of happiness or fun. It was only when we were reminded that we remembered that we had even played games. As we relived these difficult memories, we all asked the same questions: Why did so much suffering fall in our laps? Why didn't we get the joys and opportunities that every child is entitled to? So well did the poisons of casteism, classism, communalism and sexism blend into each other that their bitterness remains intact on our tongues even after all these years.

Fragmented Childhoods

In 1971, Radha was born in Unnao district in a small village called Mehrauli. As the only Paasi family in this village, Radha's family had to work hard to meet the demands of the stomach. Kurmis were the dominant caste. Out of fear of the Kurmis, several Paasi families had left their homes and formed a small settlement outside the village. Radha's father was a stubborn man. He refused to leave his own home and village. We can call his stubbornness courage, but his children paid the price for his choice. The villagers did not allow them to forget for a minute that they were untouchable.

On the day when Radha was born, there was no food at home. To take care of her own and her newborn's hunger, Amma lay little Radha on the *med* of a Kurmi's farm and collected *seela*. The grain that was left behind to rot in the field became the source of survival for Radha and her family. When she was a little older, village folk always pointed at Radha and commented: "Isn't she the one whose mother used to put her on the *med* and pick *seela*?"

When there was no grain at home, Radha's family lived on a drink made of *rab*. Radha can never forget the terror of her father—how little things provoked him into beating her mother, or forcibly mixing water in the *rab* set aside for her, and how her father's presence always terrorized Radha into silence or made her cry with fear every time he opened his mouth.

Growing up in the village's only Dalit family, Radha constantly struggled with the chains of untouchability. She could not understand why people didn't let her touch their utensils or allow her to appear in their kitchens. Why did they stop her from playing with their children? And when she somehow found a chance to play with them, why did she get beaten in her own home?

Amma always fretted about work. She didn't get a moment to breathe. But no matter how worried or busy she was, Amma took out some time every day to put some *kaajal* and oil on Radha, dress her up, and she always made sure to put a *sutiya* around Radha's neck. Neighbours often made fun when they saw this; they said: "Look at the way Radha's mother dolls her up! No one can tell that she is a Paasi."

The wounds inflicted by untouchability multiplied when Radha started school. Her father's stubbornness and pride refused to bend before the Kurmis and he sent his two daughters and three sons to study. Members of the upper castes found it unbearable that a Dalit family could also see the dream of seeking education. They taunted, "Why does this Paasi man waste so much money on his children's schooling? Why is he trying to become like the Sawarn Hindus? His sons will become labourers when they grow up. His daughters will cut grass and wash and clean for others. It would be more appropriate for him to teach them skills that they can use later!"

There was no respite inside the school either. Sawarn schoolmasters did not eat or drink from vessels touched by Radha. Once when a schoolmaster asked Radha to bring him some drinking water, Radha's joy knew no bounds. She told her mother as soon as she reached home, "Today Munshiji drank water from my hands."

At that time, the title of "Panditji" was reserved for Brahmin teachers who taught in primary schools of the villages. Teachers from other castes were referred to as "Munshiji."

It was precisely this inequality of naming that Madhulika opened her eyes to as a little girl growing up in a Raidas family in the Manpur village of Shahjahanpur district. Madhulika, whose father was a teacher, could not begin to see why people called her father

"Munshiji" when all the other schoolteachers were referred to as "Panditji." At the time of Madhulika's birth, there was a fight over land in which her father was injured. The blame for this mishap was heaped on Madhulika: "All this happened because of this girl's arrival. Things would have been better if she had died."

Having given birth to five girls, Madhulika's mother never got any relief from the jeering comments in her *sasural.* Adding to the pain of mothering five daughters, was the untimely death of Madhulika's Nani, which left Madhulika's mother burdened with the responsibility of raising her young siblings. Madhulika's youngest Mama and Mausi came to live with her mother, and Madhulika's father had to bear all their expenses as well. For this reason, despite some farming and her father's job as a schoolteacher, financial hardships continued for Madhulika's family.

"We have five daughters! How much can we do? And from where will we find the means to do everything that we are required to do for them?" These were the words that Madhulika heard over and over again from her father's mouth.

Even so, Amma managed to shower some love and affection on her daughters. Madhulika remembers how her heart leaped with joy on the days when mother warmed up some water to give her a bath or braided her hair as she got ready. Her brother's objections did not stop Amma from buying colourful bangles for her daughters with great interest and excitement.

Madhulika's experiences of casteism were quite different from Radha's. In Manpur, Madhulika's family had its own farm and its own drinking water well. Raidas formed the majority caste, and the economic status of the Brahmins was quite poor. Madhulika never felt that she was from a lower or Dalit caste. She learned that Brahmins were considered superior and Raidas were inferior in the caste hierarchy, but she always felt that "we Raidas are much better off than the Brahmins. They have nothing."

If we place the pieces of Madhulika and Radha's lives next to each other, we can see how varied the meanings of being Dalit can be for different families. Whereas the term "untouchable" appeared early on in Radha's life in the form of a painful humiliation, it mostly remained a hollow word for Madhulika.

She heard about the politics of "high born" and "low born," but the manner in which values associated with high and low are stuffed inside every pore of a Dalit family is a pain that remained largely unfamiliar to Madhulika.

When we weave the strands of Sandhya and Garima's lives in the same thread, we realize how deep and complicated this web of caste system is, as well as the process of internalizing it from the innocence of early childhood—sometimes in the name of purity, and at others in the name of self-restraint, fasts and religious rituals.

"So much was there and everything vanished." This is the grief that repeatedly haunts Sandhya's heart. Sandhya was born in 1968 in the Brahmin-dominated village of Sujanpur in Unnao district. The day of her birth was the last day of Navratri and a *havan* was taking place to mark the auspicious occasion. The birth of a girl ruined the ceremony for some. "She has made the home impure", when Sandhya's grandfather tried to stop the *havan* with this declaration, her father, who was a doctor in a government hospital, opposed it. He said, "This is a happy occasion. The *havan* must go on."

This daughter who had come after five sons was named Abha by her father—the *abha* or radiance of her five brothers! And the old grandma from the neighbourhood lovingly called her *Pachcho*! But within six months, Abha's father was killed in a riot by people from his own village.

After her father's murder, Baba announced—"Now there is only darkness. She can no longer be called Abha. Her name will be Sandhya (evening)."

Encapsulated in her new name, the grief of her father's loss became a raw wound for Sandhya. Baba always regarded Sandhya as the cause of his son's death. Raised on the fear and hatred of her father's killers within the four walls of her home, Sandhya's growing up largely went unnoticed by her extended family.

Educating five sons and a daughter was a massive challenge for Sandhya's mother. Surrounded by economic hardships and burdened by the expectations of respectability, this young Brahmin widow was forced to become completely dependent on her Sasur and Jeth. Sandhya was sent for her schooling to her uncle's house in Unnao, where as a ten-year old, she became seriously ill with a boil near her ear. There was no hope of her remaining alive. Everyone said, "She has a cancerous wound in her ear. She won't survive."

Sandhya did not get adequate nutrition because everyone felt that there was no point in feeding a girl who was destined to die. When Sandhya's stubborn body refused to succumb, her family said: "Neither will she die, nor will she relieve us!"

In these conditions, the pain of her father's loss became more and more acute for Sandhya. Deep inside, she grieved: "Why did I live if my father had to go?" Endless torture, insults and lack of care made Sandhya more rebellious with every passing day—whatever she decided to do, she didn't rest until she did it. Sandhya could not tolerate the idea of dressing and dolling herself up like other girls. So on the days of special festivals, when her mother insisted on beautifying her, Sandhya took everything off and threw it away. Since Amma's status as a widow prevented her from dressing up or making herself attractive in any way, Sandhya never got socialized into these sorts of feminine projects. All the same, we sometimes wonder if the difficult circumstances of her childhood that allowed her disinterest, stubbornness and insuppressible anger to ripen also caused Sandhya to grow distant from a whole range of feelings and processes later on in her life.

Born near Lucknow in a village called Manoharpur, Garima's circumstances were similar. Baba was the only brother among seven sisters, and he was very fond of sons. Before Garima was born, her mother had a son who died at the age of eight months. All the members of the household, along with Garima's ill grandfather, were eagerly waiting for another son to replace the dead one. When the news of a girl's birth reached them, Baba announced: "Turn off the lights. Darkness has entered."

These were Baba's last words.

Little Garima, who was responsible for filling her Baba's last moments with darkness, enjoyed very few moments of laughter and smiles. Youngest among four brothers, Garima's father was a severe alcoholic. Baba was well aware of this problem. He feared that his son would drown everything in alcohol. So after distributing hundred *beegha* of land to each of his sons and forty to each of his daughters-in-law, he gave an extra twenty *beegha* to Garima's mother so that in the event of a crisis, she would never have to beg. Baba also gave her a house in which Garima's mother lives to this day.

As a little girl, Garima watched her drunk father hammer her mother every other day. He looked for excuses to beat her. Lying drunk at home had become routine. There were phases, sometimes of more than fifteen days in a row, when Pitaji started drinking as soon as he rose from bed and drank for the entire day. He continued like this until he fell ill. All the expenses of the household, including his alcohol, were met by farming. As long as grain was stored in the house, Pitaji sold it for alcohol without a care. To meet the family's requirements, Garima's mother often sent her secretly to sell grain. Sometimes, Amma hid away a sack or two of rice, peanuts and *daal* so that her children wouldn't starve even if everything was gone.

Memories of such moments erupt as deep pangs in Garima's heart.

One day there was nothing to eat at home. Just some very old *daal*—that's all! When Amma cooked that old *daal* and sat down to quell her hunger with her three children, they saw hundreds of pests floating on the surface. All the *daal* had to be thrown away.

Another time, Garima went with her little brother and sister to eat at a neighbour's *shraddh*. She couldn't focus on eating without the thought of Amma's hunger tearing at her heart: "There is no food at home. What will Amma eat?" She hid two *pooris* in her frock and put them in her mother's hands when she reached home. Amma was not able to stop her tears for a long time.

Although hunger caused Garima to steal in her childhood, she is proud of the fact that this did not become a habit. However, her mother's deep religious inclination as well as a desire to rid herself from wounds inflicted by poverty ignited a devotion towards God in Garima's heart. She often thought that God must be there, otherwise how could the world go on? At the young age of twelve, Garima began fasting on every Thursday, Friday, and on the Mondays of *Saavan*. At the time of the *pooja* she narrated all her pains and worries to God.

Her father's alcoholism which pulled Garima towards religion, also introduced her to the many complexities of caste and casteism in her society. Pitaji used to hang out and drink with men of all castes. It was common for Garima to go into the Raidas settlement to fetch her father back home after his drinking sessions. She remembers the day when Naththoo Chamar was sitting by her house and when Garima referred to him by this name, Pitaji scolded her: "He is older than you!"

Garima writes—"This taught me to respect people from lower castes. But it could not rid me of the casteism that was ingrained in me by this time."

Both parents wanted Garima to study, so she started going to school. Sometimes when Pitaji was not at home, Garima went outside with her doll to play. But Garima's memory keeps dragging her back to the times when her own worries as a child became inseparable from the worries of her mother. Every waking moment, Garima was wrapped in the same thought: "What can I do to save Amma from Pitaji's beating today?"

Chaandni's head also fills up with similar images at the mention of childhood—Abbu's alcohol, a drunk Abbu hitting and screaming at Amma, and Amma's own suppressed anger boiling over and spilling itself on Chaandni's own little body. In the Ranipur settlement in Unnao district, Chaandni was born into a family of weavers. Her father also sold fabric. The work of weaving was done almost entirely by Amma and her three daughters. The survival of the household depended on this labour.

As a labourer struggling hard to make ends meet, Chaandni's Abbu did not receive the news of his third daughter's birth well. He was driven crazy with shock. Seeing her husband's fury, an enraged Amma sat down to work at the loom within a few hours of delivering Chaandni. She said, "What's the use of such a daughter. She is better dead than alive."

Amma became ill as a result of this difficult labour she undertook right after giving birth. She did not receive any treatment or care. But Chaandni was destined to live despite all this. So she did.

Both of Chaandni's older sisters had poor eyesight, so they could not do the finer work. Parents feared that Chaandni would also have the same problem. But when they discovered that her vision was better, their affection for this third daughter increased somewhat. When she sits down to recall the beautiful times spent with Amma, the swings of Saavan and the *Ramleela* of her village dance before Chaandni's eyes. Every year, Chaandni went to see the Ramleela with her mother. On the days when Ravana's effigy was to be burned, Amma hurriedly finished all the work at home and took off with her daughters—she always wanted to be sure that they didn't miss a single moment of the show. Similarly, during the month of Saavan, Amma loved to swing with her three daughters. Seeing her mother happy drove Chaandni wild with delight. She felt as if her Amma wanted to drown all her sorrows in the green songs of Saavan.

As she grew up around the loom, Chaandni managed to study Arabic and Farsi. Amma was eager for her third daughter to go to school since poor vision had completely prevented her other two daughters from receiving any education. Chaandni herself was dying to learn Hindi. However, the neighbours convinced her parents to keep her away from school: "In our religion, it is a sin to teach Hindi. And even otherwise, why do you want to send your girl to school when you don't want her to go out and get a job later on? She will become immoral."

Amma ordered Chaandni to sit at home and study Islam. That day, little Chaandni cried for hours. When Amma asked her to eat, she didn't even look at the food. The Pathan girls next door went to school. They were impressed by Chaandni's stubbornness and her desire to learn. They talked to Amma and tried to convince her to send Chaandni to their school. Amma agreed. Eventually, Abbu enrolled Chaandni into Kanya Junior High School. It gave Amma infinite satisfaction to see her daughter become educated. She would fill with pride and joy whenever someone came to Chaandni with a request to read out a letter. After fifth grade, there was another set of attempts to stop her education, but with Amma's support and her own drive, Chaandni successfully finished junior high school.

But the journey in other areas of life didn't turn out to be as simple as the trip to the eighth grade.

Out of the eleven teachers who taught in the Kanya Junior High School, only two were Muslims—the rest were Hindu. For her cooking exam in grade six, Chaandni worked very hard to make *zarda*. All the Hindu teachers adoringly ate the dishes cooked by other girls, but didn't even touch the food that Chaandni and her six Muslim friends cooked. Only Muslim teachers tasted Chaandni's *zarda*. Every time there was a cooking exam, something like this happened. During one exam, Chaandni bought some *mithai* and fruits and placed them on the table. When on Ustani Bahanji's request a Brahmin teacher distributed them, everyone ate without hesitation. Chaandni was restless. Next day she asked a teacher called Munni, "If you can eat *mithai* and fruits bought by me, why do you say 'stay away' when I come near you?" By ignoring Chaandni's question and sternly asking her to get lost, Munni Bahanji succeeded in driving Chaandni away from her. But she couldn't rid Chaandni's mind of the thousand questions that this incident had triggered.

Shikha, who was born in the Pratapnagar settlement, also of Unnao district, was wrapped up in a different set of concerns. She could not understand why her mother beat her so much. The thought of her mother's beating always made Shikha connect her own sorrow to a story she read in the fourth grade, that of Rakhi, who is always tortured by her stepmother. Shikha wondered: "Is it possible that my mother beats me so much because she is actually my stepmother?"

Shikha was the third daughter to be born in her family. This was her mother's second marriage. When her mother's oldest daughter was still an infant, her first husband was murdered. Shikha's father had been a widower.

Why did Maa hit Shikha so much? Was it because of the wounds from her own past, or was there something else? Little Shikha could not tell which frustrations had seated themselves so deep inside the heart of her youthful mother. When a son was born four years after Shikha's birth, her own value increased. Everyone said, "It's a good fortune that she brought a brother after herself. What would have happened if she had brought a sister?"

Pitaji used to sell traditional herbs and medicines, but his business was gradually slowing down and the economic hardships at home were growing from bad to worse. When Shikha was studying in the eighth grade, Pitaji passed away. The burden of upper caste respectability and honour—which had imprisoned the women inside the four walls of home, and chained them with a thousand restrictions suddenly disappeared, and with it vanished the pressures of hiding the hardships in order to maintain a clean and respectable image before the world.

Shikha's childhood ended on the day her father died. In one day, she aged a decade!

The environment where Pallavi learned to breathe was remote from this world of respectability and honour. In 1972, in the Bitholi village of Shahjahanpur district, Pallavi was born in a family that was struggling to make ends meet. Around the time she was born, her father was reading a novel whose heroine was called Pallavi. It is hard to tell which qualities of this heroine made her father enamoured of her, but it was after her that Pallavi was named.

In the early days of childhood, several incidents happened that left a deep mark on Pallavi's tender heart. Six days before she was born, their house caught fire. Nothing was left behind in a house that had been put together with a great deal of hard labour. Pallavi grew up with everyone blaming her: "This *karamjali* ended everything even before she arrived."

When she was just six months old, a wolf came into the house and grabbed Pallavi in its mouth. Who knows how this happened, but the family's pet dog chased the wolf and Pallavi fell out from the mouth of the fleeing wolf. The wounds that this accident left on Pallavi's body healed with medication, but several other injuries that she had in her young life still remain raw.

Wasn't she only nine years old when Mishraji from her neighbourhood started tempting Pallavi with biscuits and candies to come and spend time with him? When Pallavi came near him, he forcibly touched and stroked her and said, "Everyone does this. Your parents do it too."

When Pallavi told Amma, her mother screamed at her, "Who asked you to go near that filthy man?"

Filled with disgust and hatred for Mishraji, Pallavi was silenced by her mother's scolding. But as she grew older, she learned better and better how voices of girls like herself were snatched away as soon as they began to speak—so that men like Mishraji could fearlessly play whatever games they wanted to with their bodies.

The Blending of Seven Childhoods

In this entire collective journey of writing, no other phase of our lives made us shed more tears than when we poured out our childhoods on paper. In the day-to-day thrashings of our everyday life, we had nearly forgotten that a childhood even existed in our past. But when we dug out our tiny bags of childhood, and carefully cleared the layers of dust that had accumulated on them, memories pierced our fingertips like sharp-edged stones.

Many pains and injuries were buried there, but when we connected the stories of our seven lives we repeatedly found ourselves tied with the thick rope of casteism, sometimes at opposite ends. There was no denying that each one of us had suffered deprivation, but the ways in which caste-based violence shapes, deepens and poisons that deprivation became the theme of our discussions.

This talk was not so easy for us to engage in. It was difficult for some of us to accept that even in the midst of our poverty, the very accident of birth in an upper caste had made our survival far easier than others. The pain of hunger is the same for all children, but the circumstances and means by which that hunger is satisfied make one child's hunger different than another's. How can we not distinguish between a circumstance where there is nothing to eat or cook in one home and the mother has to lay her newborn baby on the edge of someone's farm to pick up the remains from a harvested field, and another situation where, despite many problems, a mother is able to save a few lentils, peanuts, and rice to feed her hungry children? But even here, the irony is that she can save the grain from her alcoholic husband but not from the pests. And then, again, we find that a starved Brahmin girl gets an opportunity to kill her family's hunger by stealing food at a neighbour's death ceremony, whereas a Dalit girl in her place could have only hoped to find some leftovers after the caste Hindus had thrown away their plates on the street.

To have a purely intellectual conversation on such differences is one thing, but grappling with them through personal writing is quite another. Those of us who are Sawarn often felt that we were quite sensitive to the issue of caste, and so we could feel the pain experienced by a Dalit. This made Sandhya say once that we can all feel the pain of casteism because each of us has seen it closely. At this point, Radha calmly reminded Sandhya: "To feel someone's pain is one thing, and living that pain is another. You might have felt it, but some of us have lived it. Your experiences cannot be the same as mine."

Pallavi repeated the saying in Awadhi:

Jake paaon na phate bevai
So kya jaane peer parai
(Those whose feet don't get cracks in them
Can barely begin to understand another's pain)

But even when they crack, do all feet crack in the same way? Aren't caste politics constantly twisted around and complicated by class- and place-based circumstances? Even though Madhulika ranks lower in the caste hierarchy than Radha, she grew up in a context where the Sawarn castes were neither rich, nor did they dominate numerically. The shadow of hunger and humiliation under which Radha grew up was entirely unimaginable for Madhulika as a child.

The untouchability and social marginalization that Radha experienced were connected, along with acute poverty, to her family's status as the only Dalit family residing in the village. On top of that, her father's rebellious challenge to the so-called superiority of upper castes further complicated the circumstances of Radha's childhood. The insults hurled at her every day paralyzed Radha's tongue.

Sandhya, too, became quiet as a result of the insults and indifference that she suffered after her father's death. But even as she endured the blame for her father's murder, Sandhya's status as a Brahmin also convinced her that she was superior and more pure than others. Perhaps it is due to these complexities of class, caste and social environment that Sandhya acquired a new voice and fury to rebel when she grew up, whereas Radha learned to become quiet in the middle of conflict. Radha does not feel that it is always necessary for her to be heard or listened to. That listening to her would enable upper caste people to understand or accept her point of view is a hope that Radha stopped holding on to long ago.

Another moving theme in our conversations was our ability to connect with the pains and desires of our mothers and grandmothers.

Chaandni wondered if her mother's rage at the time of her birth was related to the fact that Abbu had an intimate relationship with another woman at that time. Perhaps Amma was worried that an unwanted child would push her husband even farther away from her, increasing the torture that was inflicted on her everyday.

Similarly, when the mothers of Sandhya and Garima became widowed at the age of 26 and 28, respectively, what must have been their circumstances, their struggles, their needs and desires? In the world we breathed in, we learned early on to accept men's sexual desires as their requirements. Several of us even came to know about the relationships that our own fathers had with other women. But why could we never think about the sexual needs and desires of our mothers?

As we recalled the violence inflicted on our mothers, some of us were also gripped by the tearful memories of our grandmothers' sufferings. Garima's grandmother was beaten so mercilessly by her husband for years that she had turned permanently blue below her waist. As she was writing her diary, Garima wondered about the nature of her grandparent's relationship. She never felt that her Baba had any softness or love for her Dadi. If Baba gave farms to all his sons and daughters-in-law, why couldn't he give some land to Dadi as well? After dedicating her entire body and soul to her home, family and husband throughout her life, Dadi couldn't even count on anyone to offer her some food in her last days.

While writing our diaries, our own sorrows entwined so tightly with those of our mothers and grandmothers that it was no longer possible for us to separate them. As we reflected on the lives of our mothers, it also became clear to us how in the struggles of our lives, our wealth and poverty, our religion and caste, and our status as women all remain entangled with each other. For instance, if a Raidas is wealthy, his woman will also remain inside *purdah* in the name of honour and respectability no matter how much she is beaten and tortured there. Garima's mother was aware that her husband would not beat her if she stepped out of the house. Yet, she remained so imprisoned in the definitions of familial honour that she spent her whole youth suffocating inside the walls of her home. She willingly accepted that stepping out of the house would bring disgrace to her family, even though the whole village knew that she was beaten inhumanly inside that house. Why didn't she think of that violence as a familial disgrace? What kinds of social values and environment taught her to suffer torture, but not to resist? To accept imprisonment, but not to choose a way out?

A third issue that made us nervous was religion and communal violence. Each time Sandhya tearfully recalled that murderous night when her father was slaughtered, we were reminded of the riots in Gujarat, and other riots like the one in Gujarat. Sandhya was only six months old when her father was killed—yet she always thought of taking revenge on his murderers. Then, what must happen to the minds of children who are forced to witness the burning bodies of their fathers, the chopped-up corpses of their brothers, or the gang rapes and collective torture of their mothers and sisters? What kind of fire must burn inside them year after year? How many unshed tears must they be accumulating with every passing year?

The destruction of the Babri mosque shook Chaandni in a similar way when people in her village began to fight without any reason. After the tragedy of the Babri mosque, there were rumours in the village that the village mosque was going to be broken today...tomorrow... In the middle of all this, a Bhangi man killed a pig and left its corpse on the steps of the mosque. Violence erupted and the Bhangi was killed. The conspiracy must have been hatched by someone else but it was the Bhangi who had to lose his life—because it was his hands that were forced to commit the act of leaving an animal that has been considered *haraam* in Islam.

These are the kind of circumstances that make Chaandni's life and work more challenging than the rest of the group's. On the one hand, she has to maintain the courage to carry on social struggles in an environment filled with communal misunderstandings and hatred. On the other hand, she has to tolerate the accusations from her own people that her work and behaviour are like that of Hindus. How, despite all of this, does Chaandni manage to remain so calm and balanced? How does she continue to create and recite beautiful couplets and poetry?

When we first sat down to talk about our childhoods, we learned that five out of seven of us had cursed our own birth—Why were we born? Why did so much suffering fall in our tiny laps? When we started reading our diaries to each other, we felt that the suffering we endured in our childhoods formed the most critical link that connected each of our lives. But as our conversations deepened, we realized that there was much more that remained to be said and shared. So much of the discussion inside women's NGOs is focused on gender based violence, but the thoroughness and completeness with which that violence is entangled and stuck in the violence of casteism, communalism and class politics is something that we have hardly paid attention to in our past meetings, workshops and field work. The way all these forms of violence get mingled, blended and roped into each other; the degree to which these entangled structures of violence are rooted in our histories and present contexts; and the ways in which these understandings of our violent pasts and present must inform our future battles—these are the issues in which we have decided to immerse ourselves... So that twenty years from now, if our daughters sit down like us to remember and write about their childhoods, they will be able to share not just tears but also colourful moments of fun, adventure and laughter... And so that none of them feels forced to write a single word that curses her own birth.

From the Streets of Babul to the Wetness of *Aanchal*

I was nice and plump to look at. I used to think that if I were a boy, I would have found myself a job. My dream was to have a [salaried] job. Two of my sisters had been married off. They were tormented in their *sasurals*—they wouldn't get a piece of clothing even in three-four years. I often wondered that my father was a schoolmaster; then why did he marry off his daughters like this? I just prayed that whomever I got to marry would have a regular job and lots of money. I dreamed of living with my husband in the city. I didn't want to live like my sisters...and I never wanted to visit my *mayaka* without my husband beside me...

— From Madhulika's diary

Ever since our work has connected us to women's lives, it has almost become a daily routine for us to confront incidents of domestic and social violence. From the time we first become aware of our youth until all our hair turn grey, it seems that all poor women go through the same kind of pain. First, we all become burdens in our *mayakas*; then, we suffer humiliations in our *sasurals*, get beaten, stay hungry; and our bodies become someone else's property...So thoroughly do we get wrapped in these sorrows that sometimes it is hard for us to turn back and reflect on the dreams that we had once seen and nurtured so keenly, so fervently. It is true that many of our dreams were never realized, or were crushed; but as we write and share our stories today, we realize that the dreams we see at each turn of our lives teach us a great deal about possibilities, absences, struggles and challenges.

So stealthily did the pains and joys of our childhood turn into pangs and dreams of adolescence that we were caught unaware. But when we sat down to remember, we recalled how the changes in our own bodies filled us with the excitement and fear of adventure and discovery. On top of that were all those desires and dreams that started swelling within us like waves as we reached adolescence and simply refused to be tamed.

With these, came the ever-increasing strictness with which our elders controlled and monitored us, the never-ending remarks and interference of the entire world, the teasing by young men, and the suffocation of new rules and regulations that were imposed on us every day. Madhulika and Pallavi vividly recall the day when their fathers had commented angrily to their mothers, "Tell her to cover herself with a *dupatta* when she moves around!"

Later, a relative threatened Madhulika, "If you don't learn how to cook properly, we won't come to save you even if they kill you in your *sasural.*"

Once after cooking the day's meal, Pallavi left for school and forgot to insist that her mother should eat. Amma didn't eat anything for hours and later admonished Pallavi: "How will you survive in your *sasural* if you behave like this? What is your standing, after all? You will be burned alive if you don't do better than this."

The more we liked to doll ourselves up in those days, the more it made our elders nervous. We couldn't figure out how our very same Ammas who fed their own desires by doing us up when we were little now ganged up with everyone to prevent us from dressing up and looking pretty. Pallavi writes: "Amma often bought me bangles when I was small, but by the time I was ten or twelve her interference started. Whenever I insisted that I wanted new bangles, Amma and Babu repeated the same lines: 'Now you are grown up. Wear new bangles when you go to your own home [*sasural*].'"

Perhaps they were both concerned about what people would say if they saw their adolescent daughter all decked up. And who would pay the price if she became the object of someone's desire?

Similarly, Radha remembers the day when she first painted her nails. Her father got so furious that she had to instantly scrape it all off with a razor.

The dreams of youth were not so easily chased away by these threats and scoldings, however. We had dreams that we would study a lot and get jobs for ourselves, that we would fall in love and marry young men we loved, that our husbands would be good-looking men with salaried jobs who would spoil us rotten with love. We imagined a home in town, and if not that, at the very least we looked forward to having a tiny room of our own where we could sit with our love and talk to our heart's content...

But where did our parents have the means to pay the fat dowries that would have bought us such husbands? All of us had become burdens to our families. Today, we wonder why, if our circumstances were so full of absences and deprivations, did we wish for jewellery and clothes, employed husbands, and urban lives? Another question that bewilders us is: Why wasn't a single one of us able to associate the dreams of our youth with a peasant, farmer or labourer?

Now we recognize how terribly these dreams of our unripened age were caught up in the politics of class, wealth, social status and respectability. After seeing our married sisters and sisters-in-law we concluded that the young women whose husbands have jobs in town, who have fancy jewellry and clothes to show off, are the ones who are held in high esteem when they return to their *mayaka*; they are welcomed and treated to fancy feasts and foods. In contrast, when a wife of a peasant or manual labourer returns to her mother's home, people make a face. The already low status of the girl drops down a couple more notches.

In these circumstances, our dreams were destined to shatter. But how could we have known that? We found out only when the glass castles that we had so laboriously constructed with our sleepless eyes and tossing and turning bodies started breaking into pieces right before us.

And one of us did not even dream any dreams. When the rest of us read our diaries on youth, Sandhya remained silent. Not just then. The same Sandhya who wants to state her opinions very excitedly and stubbornly about everything, became quiet every time the subject of love or sexuality came up. She even wrote in her diary once: "I feel suffocated every time there is a conversation on sexuality, intimacies between women and men or *samlaingikta* (same-sex sexuality). I just want them to shut their mouths up...My husband also worries why I am always avoiding these subjects."

Why did Sandhya turn away from feelings that are often regarded as natural processes of sexuality by the time she reached adolescence? It is difficult for Sandhya to figure out whether it was the overwhelming and all-consuming shock of her father's murder that was responsible for this withdrawal, or whether it was something else. The thing that she does know with certainty is that she never dreamed a single dream of love, romance or marriage. Whenever the topic of weddings or marriage came up, she just prayed that no man should ever agree to marry her. She was convinced that if she could manage not to marry, her brothers would never have to plead before anyone on her account.

If youth were associated just with our seen and unseen dreams and the pain of their shattering and breaking, things might have been a bit easier for us...but our agony was increased by all the horrors that stood gaping before us at every turn. Every day new fears and panics were created for us—sometimes it was the fear of menstruation, and at others it was the fear of familial disgrace that would come from not being married before the onset of menstruation. Sometimes we dreaded looking beautiful, and at others we were frightened of the consequences of falling in love against social restrictions. Relatives from our caste and clan also missed no opportunity to explain to us that it is our society's business to place countless question marks on the character of women, and the accused woman has absolutely no right to contradict or interrogate those accusations. With this, the world was also doing a good job of demonstrating to us that a woman without a husband only gets a place on the margins of our society, whether her husband has been snatched by death, or whether she has herself chosen to reject matrimony.

Whenever Madhulika sat down to write about the early days of her youth, she always remembered how her first consciousness of youth came only with fear. When at the age of ten, she had to walk two kilometres from her home to school, the boys she met on the way said vulgar things and cracked crude jokes. When she went to junior high school, there too, she saw lust in the eyes of the schoolmaster. For a plump, playful, happy-go-lucky Madhulika, the early arrival of puberty became a curse. Everyone started meddling and intervening in the energetic games she played with the boys in her neighbourhood. When she did not pay attention to newly-imposed rules, she was beaten. Similarly, her open laughter became a prickly thorn for everybody. There were serious complaints about her laughing too much. Once something made her laugh really hard when she was giving water to the bulls; her older brother, who was watching, punished her by thrashing her soundly.

Madhulika did not like household chores. She dreamed of working for the police one day. She loved to play, fool around, and create a commotion everywhere. She wanted to breathe fresh air but every time she tried to do it she was beaten—sometimes by her mother, sometimes by her older sister, and sometimes by her brother. Madhulika wondered why suddenly there were restrictions on her leaving the house? What was so criminal about roaring with laugher?

She began to find the answers one day when an unmarried woman in her village was killed and Bhabhi explained to her, "That girl spent a lot of time with boys. She had a bad character. That's why she was killed." Madhulika was petrified on hearing Bhabhi's words. A deep shock made her promise to herself that she was never going to talk to any boy again, because otherwise people will assume that she was immoral and wrong. She decided to focus all her hopes on marrying a nice-looking, salaried young man one day.

Standing on the threshold of youth, a bright-eyed Chaandni also filled colours in a thousand dreams. It did not take much time for these colourful images to fade away, however. Like Madhulika, Chaandni also learned rather quickly about the many poisons that were determined to wipe out her dreams.

Chaandni loved to play with make-up. Once, while putting kohl in her eyes, she made a little black mole on her chin. Amma saw this, and beat her mercilessly. But Amma's thrashings could not restrain Chaandni's heart. She just looked forward to a life after marriage when there would be no restrictions on looking beautiful. She would get decked up in pretty clothes and jewellery, and no one would stop her from being fashionable and wearing fancy things.

Chaandni's Abbu loved to hang out with her Mamu. They were drinking buddies. Close to their home was a *purva* that was known for sex-trade. Abbu was intimate with one of the women there. Perhaps this was also one of the main reasons behind the physical abuse that Amma suffered everyday.

Mamu accompanied Abbu to the *purva* sometimes. Once when Amma found out that Mamu had slept with a Raidas woman, she yelled furiously at him. Later, the same Mamu complained to Abbu that Abbu's own sister (Chaandni's Phoophi) was having an affair with a boy in the neighbourhood. Chaandni was too young to figure out the details of what and how things happened to Phoophi after this incident. All she knows is that both brothers took Phoophi to a doctor on some pretense and asked him to administer her a poisonous injection. Phoophi died. The family remained silent about this murder.

This tragedy shook Chaandni. When Mamu had sex with a woman, he simply got screamed at, but when Phoophi fell in love, she had to give up her life.

Perhaps it was because of Phoophi's death that extra chains were thrown around Chaandni and her sisters. When young men made vulgar cracks at them in the streets, her heart filled with horror at the thought of what might happen if her mother found out about it. Battered and maltreated by Abbu, Amma used to take out her frustration by beating her three daughters. She hit so hard that the girls bled.

When Chaandni was about ten or eleven, Amma and Abbu arranged her engagement with a boy who worked in Abbu's shop. This fellow always looked for opportunities to have fun with Chaandni. Along with Amma and Abbu, this husband-to-be now became Chaandni's third patrol. Night and day, he kept a strict eye on her. He did whatever pleased him with Chaandni's body. If Chaandni protested, he remarked, "After all, I am the one who will marry you."

He did not care one whit what Chaandni thought or wanted.

Like Chaandni, Garima's heart was also soaring high. Her eyes were dreamy. She loved to dress up. Garima's widowed mother was always anxious about her oldest daughter who had come of age and was fast becoming a woman. A village girl had fallen in love with one of Garima's cousins. When there was opposition to this relationship, the girl ate poison and died. A few days later, her lover also committed suicide. This horrified Garima's mother. With folded hands and bent knees, she begged Garima, "Beti, I will worship your feet (marry you off) whenever you ask me to. Just don't bring any dishonour to the family."

Garima could almost touch the fear that was making her mother's voice tremble. It gave her soaring heart a pause. She felt waves of desire rising within her when she watched good-looking boys, but she also learned quickly to tame her feelings and bring them back to the ground. When she was seventeen or eighteen, Garima became infatuated with a friend's brother. Even in the blistering heat of the summer, that boy used to wait for Garima on the terrace everyday. But before the romance could proceed any further, Garima's mother discovered them, and Garima was shipped off to her Nani's house in no time.

Suffocating under the restrictions of a widowed mother and of past wealth and glory, Shikha found herself in somewhat similar circumstances. Whenever she tried to form her adolescent dreams, her mother's image appeared before her eyes. She was forced to erase every dream from her heart's slate before she could even complete the sketch. When the conditions at home deteriorated after her father's death, Shikha became completely silent. A quiet Shikha came to be known as a nice, gentle and cultured girl in her society.

But her heart was not so silent; Shikha desperately wished to marry a good-looking, salaried man. She had a young male neighbour who had a job. Whenever she saw him, her imagination took off: "I wish my mother would fix me up with this boy." But it was not so easy to express these feelings to her mother. Nor was Shikha ever able to muster the courage to do so.

Out of all seven of us, Radha was the only one who was lucky enough to find a companion of her choice. She was able to do so because she had the full support of her father.

The anxieties that the arrival of womanhood brought for Radha were more intense than Shikha's. She was always worried about the lustful eyes of upper caste men; for this reason, she never went to school alone. Along with the other injuries and humiliations, the only Dalit family in the village was forced to accept this new burden of its daughters' youth. They were always concerned that if there was any kind of dishonourable act of violence against Radha or her sister, their already poor conditions would deteriorate.

By the time she reached the seventh grade, Radha's thoughts turned to wedding and *sasural*. Once, her best friend Kiran excitedly began to arrange Radha's marriage with a boy in their school. It was all done in play, but when Radha's mother found out, she struck Radha and screamed at her.

In many ways, Radha remained in fear of her father; as a little girl, almost anything he did or said made her breakdown. But somehow his open ideas about marriage had a profound influence on Radha. He often said, "In the city, girls marry by choice these days. If you ever feel attached to someone, you should always tell your family."

God knows how the same father who so cruelly beat Amma became so generous when it came to his daughters' marriage, but his influence created an atmosphere where Radha and her sister could gather the courage to talk openly about their likes and dislikes in men with their father. They also began to find a voice in other related matters. Once, on the occasion of Radha's brother's wedding, when her father demanded a television and a bike in dowry, Radha snapped, "All right then, why don't you set aside two television sets and bicycles for the sisters. If you insist on taking things in your son's wedding, remember that you will also have to give your daughters the same items in their weddings."

Radha once rejected a boy who was a possible match because she found him completely unattractive. But she was really attracted to a boy from the Kurmi caste. If there were no restrictions on inter-caste marriages, she would have liked to marry him. Radha was wise enough to know that the gulfs of caste are not so easily bridged, so she did not give an inkling of her feelings to anyone at home.

Some time later, Radha fell in love with the son of a distant relative and became very attached to him. Luckily, she was able to marry the same man. But Radha could have never accomplished this feat in her community without the support of her father and brother.

Perhaps it was his personal struggle against the injustices of the caste system that made Radha's father fearless enough to depart from established social norms associated with matrimonial practices and to give his two daughters the right to choose their own life partners. But Pallavi's situation stood in stark contrast to Radha's. Fraught with the weight of caste purity, society refused to forgive Pallavi's parents for the "innocent crime" of not being able to marry off their daughter before puberty.

Pallavi was nine years old at the time of her Bhaiyya's and Didi's wedding. After that, the responsibilities of doing all the household chores fell on her little shoulders. The contempt and ridicule that Didi had to face in her *sasural* for bringing a small dowry filled Pallavi's heart with a thousand anxieties. When she reached twelve years of age, neighbours started remarking, "The girl is coming of age. Why don't you marry her off?"

It was around this time when Pallavi returned home from school one day and discovered blood stains on her clothes. She wondered whether she had a boil or cancer in her stomach. When Pallavi told Amma, she said, "This time when you go, make three dots with the same blood and then erase half of one. This is a *totka*. It will ensure that your period just comes for two and a half days. Now you are grown-up."

After three days, mother instructed Pallavi to wash her hair and said, "Every month, do the same thing."

There were new restrictions as well: Do not cook at the time you are menstruating. Do not worship the Gods. Do not water the *tulsi* plant, and so on. But even after all this, the policing did not let up. Amma started being scoffed at by neighbours for not marrying her daughter off before the onset of menstruation. Once a goat wandered over in Amma's field and Amma tied it in her yard. The woman who owned the goat came to fight. Screaming, she mocked her mother, "How dare you threaten me by capturing my goat when you could not even worship the feet of your faith" (couldn't marry your daughter off before puberty). A couple of days later, Pallavi's Babuji left the house to look for a boy.

Pallavi and Chaandni were married off at unripe ages of thirteen and fourteen. Those of us who were not married so early, however, were also imprisoned under the weight of a hundred chores and regulations. The painful strings of childhood and the knotted ropes of adolescence became thoroughly entangled in our lives. Sometimes, while writing our diaries we could not understand which moments belonged to our childhood and which to our youth. But there was one thing that we could say with certainty: the pain of the dreams that started shattering and the remnants of which got deposited in our insides, made us cry a lot more in our youth than in our childhood.

Why did you Marry me off to a Distant Land...?[1]

> Once my husband hit me very badly. I thought of going somewhere and ending my life...but he forcibly dragged me back from the street...My heart cried, "What will I do with this life...?" But then I started thinking about how my father thrashed my mother with a thick stick, and how strong she stayed in spite of all that. She suffered his beatings and continued to carry all the domestic burdens, and never thought of ending her life. As compared to her, I was such a weakling. Maybe it was true that women were created just to work...I had heard from the mouths of my elders, "Husband is God. He can do anything." So I, too, became silent . . . and tried to live like a good daughter-in-law in my *sasural*.
>
> —From Radha's diary

Sometimes we ache when we think that we did not get to fully live a piece of the dreams we had once seen. With our weddings, the dreams we had seen in adolescence started falling apart like palaces of cards. The same burdens, insults and pains that we watched being inflicted on our mothers fell upon us, too. The world had already taught us that the *sasural* was our real home, but no one had prepared us for how different the atmosphere and circumstances of that *sasural* would be from our expectations. When the time came for us to step out of the shadow of our *mayaka*, we were tormented by just one worry: Who would do all the work once we leave? Who would give a hand to our tired mothers? To the world, our mother's home may not have been our true home. Even so, the worry that gnawed at us at the time of *bidai* was, "Who would take care of things in our *mayaka* after us?"

But as soon as we reached *sasural* we found ourselves so pressured under a new set of rules, restrictions, and responsibilities that memories of the *mayaka* became sharp pangs of yearning. The hardships of childhood, the pressures of work and the limitations imposed upon us before marriage—all started seeming smaller and easier.

There was a time when we had imagined a lover and life companion in the form of a husband. But when we encountered reality we realized that we had been brought to our *sasurals* as slaves—not as ordinary slaves, but as slaves who were expected to increase the pride and status of the family by bringing fat dowries and property. As we mulled over the stories of seven lives, we became acutely aware of the fact that a wife and daughter-in-law enters her *sasural* in the form of a servant—a servant that the *sasural* can force behind *purdah* in the name of honour and pride, or who they can beat and strip naked to the world as they wish. She cannot clothe or cover herself as she wants; she cannot move in and out of the house as she wants; and she cannot share her joys and sorrows with her family in the *mayaka*. And even after scorching her heart and soul in the fire of the home night and day, she cannot rightfully ask for a stomach full of food, nor can she expect medication or care in sickness. What falls into her lap for her entire lifetime is work and only work! If she is able to seize anything else that is fulfilling for her, it is not because of society but in spite of it—just because she managed to get it by her own will.

When a happy-go-lucky Madhulika was first seen and rejected by a prospective groom, her self-respect was crushed to pieces. If she had the faintest idea that he would do this she would have said "no" before he could reject her.

Then there were attempts to find a match for her in several places. Eventually, her marriage was arranged with a young man from Hardaspur. He was a farmer and fatherless. Neither Madhulika nor her father particularly cared to match her with him, but the groom's family owned ten *beegha* of farming land, and that was significant. Plus, there was no demand for dowry.

When Madhulika's marriage was arranged, she wept inconsolably. She could not get over the reality of going into a *kuchcha* house, where her father-in-law was dead, and where the family survived on farming, with no one having a salaried job. "Who will be there to listen to me about my hardships," Madhulika thought, "How will I bear all this?"

Madhulika's brother got married five days before her. Many fancy items had been bought for her new Bhabhi—there were seven *saris* and gold earrings. Madhulika proudly thought—"I am also the daughter of a salaried man. I, too, will get all these things." But when the box of bridal gifts reached her home, there was just one pair each of ear studs and anklets, and two *saris*! Pitaji could not bear this humiliation. He threw away the gifts and screamed, "We don't want to have this wedding. Take the *barat* back!"

In an earlier ceremony of *Dwarchar*, Madhulika had seen the groom. He was ten or twelve years older than her. She wished that she did not have to marry this man. As things began to simmer, she felt like running away from the other door. Both sides kept quarreling until 2 AM. Ultimately, the wedding ceremony took place for the fear that it would bring a bad name to both families, and the *barat* departed promptly after that.

When she reached her *sasural*, Madhulika was loaded with immense work and responsibilities. She had to take care of the daily maintenance of the *kuchcha* house, she had to do all the chores from the field as well as the house, and on top of that were the never-ending contempt and taunts of her mother- and sister- in law.

As if all this were not enough, her husband could never get away from gambling. One day when he gambled and lost a thousand-rupee watch that he had received as a wedding gift,

Madhulika had a huge fight with him. Although her husband never resorted to violence, gambling became a touchy subject and led to quarrels between them every other day. Madhulika longed for her *mayaka* every time she heard the song:

> *Sukhwa ka man rahal, dukhwa mein beetal dinwa*
> (My heart had longed for happiness, but all my days are passing in sorrow)

Madhulika never said a word about her *sasural* in her *mayaka*. She remained silent about it perhaps because she had seen the life of her Bua very closely.

Bua has been living in the *mayaka* for the last fifty years. When this same Bua from a well-off *mayaka* reached her *sasural* as a teenager, she found much poverty and discrimination there. The Thakur caste was dominant in the village and her father-, brother- and sister-in-law were all manual labourers for the Thakurs. All this was very painful for Bua. One day the food that Bua cooked did not turn out well. When Saas began to fight with Bua about her cooking, Bua retorted sharply: "What you call a 'meal' in your house, is merely called 'scraps' in mine."

Bua angrily left for her *mayaka*, never to return to her *sasural* again. As long as Bua's body had strength, she got full respect in her *mayaka*. She was also given a small house to live in. But when her body got tired and her bones started creaking, no one even offered her leftover food. Madhulika always saw a glimpse of herself in her hardworking, strong-willed and proud Bua. But whenever she thought about Bua's later years, Madhulika felt sad; had Bua stayed in her *sasural*, she probably would not have suffered in this way. That is why Madhulika never talked about her marital woes to folks in her *mayaka*.

Similarly, Sandhya was relentlessly scorned in her *sasural* because of her inadequate dowry. These insults felt like swallowing blood, but Sandhya did not whisper any of this in her *mayaka* because she could not bear to see her brothers suffer on her account. After the death of her father, Sandhya's whole childhood had shrunk and revolved around her brothers. After she got married, Sandhya never wanted her brothers to be troubled because of her, no matter how many ordeals she had to undergo.

But how strange are our lives entangled in these webs of *mayaka* and *sasural*. Sometimes it was our *mayaka* that embraced us as its own, and sometimes it was our *sasural*. And sometimes, despite having these two homes, we continued to feel as if there was not a corner or place in our lives that we could truly call our own.

Like Madhulika, a loadful of woes associated with poverty and gambling also befell Radha. She could not think of any way to deal with this except to hold her tongue like Madhulika and Sandhya.

The village in which Radha arrived after marriage had a much different atmosphere than her *mayaka*. Back home, it was only her family that was called "untouchable," but here, the Paasi and Raidas lived in close quarters so the feeling of being seen as an "untouchable" was not so overwhelming. Radha felt the relief of being freed of a stigma that had chased her day and night.

If only it were so easy to escape the deep wounds inflicted by that label "untouchable"! Living among these Dalit communities, Radha felt with an unprecedented intensity the profound ways in which poverty shaped people's daily lives. The young men of these castes were the most addicted to gambling and alcoholism. Almost all the machines in the village—tractors, threshers, boring wells, flour grinders, engines, jaggery-making machines—were in the control of the Maurya caste. It was these resourceful Mauryas who also owned all of the village's wealth. There was a time when there were no machines, but everyone, including the Dalit castes, managed to eke out some sort of living. But as the numbers of machines multiply, acute starvation among the Paasi and Raidas is being accompanied by sharply increased incidences of gambling, alcoholism and internal clashes.

At the time Radha became hooked on the appearance of her prospective husband, she had no idea that he did not work. How could a man unable to take care of his own expenses bear those of a new bride? Sasur and older Devar were well known gamblers. Her husband's excuse for not working was that whatever he would earn by working outside would be eaten up by his father's and brother's gambling. Despite having fifteen *beegha* of farmland, the family was so deeply caught in the clutches of gambling that there were days when the hearth stayed cold. All the farms were mortgaged so that gambling could go on.

A lot of things were also deliberately hidden from Radha in the beginning. Her mother-in-law feared that if her new Bahu found out about the real circumstances of her new home, she might return to her *mayaka*. A rejection of the *sasural* by Radha would have crushed her mother-in-law's honour. But her Saas never paused to reflect on why she made the maintenance of familial honour solely Radha's responsibility. Wasn't the family dishonored daily before the village community by her gambling husband and son?

Only six months into the marriage, some of the utensils given to Radha in dowry were mortgaged. Radha found out about this when her husband was about to reclaim the utensils. Saas began to fight with her son—"Why did you have to share this secret with Bahu. If she discloses this in her *mayaka*, all my *izzat* would vanish." Saas was ready to strangle herself in fury.

Radha's husband made her vow that she would not breathe a word about this incident in her *mayaka*. Radha complied. But others always advised her that the conditions of her *sasural* were far from okay. She would never get any respite here. It would be better for her to leave this home and return to her *mayaka* before it was too late.

Radha's husband gave her plenty of love and affection, but he was a very suspicious man, maybe because he himself used to have intimate relationships with other women in the village. If Radha ever commented jokingly about this, she got battered. But anytime she dared to talk to another man, a huge drama ensued. Radha often thought: "By what name should I call this marriage? In reality I have given my husband and *sasural* complete rights of possession over my body."

People often say that only wealthy bourgeoisie can keep their women imprisoned behind the *purdah* because if a woman from a poor household were to sit in the *purdah*, there would be no bread to eat at home. But our experiences have taught us that this assumption is only partially true. It is true that the feet of the daughters and daughters-in-law of the so-called respectable families are chained in the name of maintaining " *khandani izzat-aabroo.*" But there is also severe *purdah* in our Dalit and poor homes—whether among the Hindus or the Muslims. That is why, like Radha, Chaandni's struggles were also intensified by the strict *purdah* of her *sasural.*

Chaandni's first *nikah* took place at the age of thirteen. At that time, she had not even started her menstrual cycle. Her first husband was the same young man who was once madly in love with her. Chaandni used to imagine a world after marriage where there would be only joy—fairs, socializing with relatives and friends, and who knows what else! But what happens is always what Khuda wishes.

In her *sasural,* too, handloom weaving was the chief source of livelihood; five to six *dhotis* had to be woven every day. Chaandni knew that new brides had to cover their faces in the *sasural.* But she could not digest the idea of hiding her face from her own relatives.

Saas used to order, "Cover yourself." But the more she insisted, the more Chaandni ignored her commands. What Chaandni had learned from her mother was that according to Islam, the *purdah* between a woman and a man was one of the eye, not of the face.

Chaandni's stubbornness angered her husband: "Do what Ammi asks you to do," he would say.

Chaandni would reply, "Those who are mine are also yours. Why should I hide my face from those who have seen me naked as a child?"

When she became obstinate on this issue in her *sasural,* matters reached a head. There was a clash between Amma (Chaandni's mother) and Saas.

Very soon, her husband also became violent. He wanted Chaandni's father to arrange a separate shop for his livelihood, but this was an impossible demand for Chaandni's poor Abbu to meet. He said, "I have other daughters to attend to as well. What will I do for them?"

Abbu's refusal resulted in intensifying Chaandni's misery. She didn't even get a belly full of food. Saas would hand her a plate with some *sabzi,* and when no one was watching she poured water even in that. Sometimes, Chaandni pleaded to her husband—"Your mother gives you more food. Can you leave a little bit for me in your plate sometimes. My stomach never gets full."

When she got sick, she got no treatment or attention—only chores! No one cared a whit about the baby growing in her womb. Within a year of her marriage, Chaandni bore a girl. Eight days before giving birth, Chaandni was beaten mercilessly. When she found out that the newborn was a girl, her heart sank.

Everyone in the house had been anticipating a boy. With the daughter's birth, a mountain of woes fell upon Chaandni. She got no food or rest. A mother at the age of fourteen, Chaandni's body gave up. When she became very ill, Amma and Abbu brought her back from her *sasural* to their own home. She went through treatment for a full month and a half.

As soon as she recovered, her husband arrived and began to threaten her, "If you want to come to my home, you will have to come now."

Chaandni was still on medication at this time. She was not prepared to go back yet. She said, "Who am I to you? You only listen to your Ammi. Go be with her. Who will take care of the expenses for me and my daughter? Who will pay for the drugs if I get sick again?"

Abbu also started crying. He said to his son-in-law, "We will never forget the way you have mistreated us."

The son-in-law retorted sharply, "Fine, then. Why don't you get a divorce?"

His words shook the earth beneath Chaandni and her parents. The day this incident occured Chaandni got a paralytic stroke in one arm and leg. Her eyesight also grew weak. It was only after Abbu spent four thousand rupees on her treatment in Kanpur city that she was able to stand up again. As soon as she got better, her husband reappeared.

Chaandni begged him, "Please give Amma some of the money they have spent on my treatment."

Her husband replied, "What money? I won't give a *paisa*. If you want to come with me, then come along. I am here only because people forced me to come. Otherwise, what I really want is a divorce."

Chaandni could not decide whether this man was her husband or her enemy. She decided not to return. What if she became pregnant again?

Abbu and Amma were extremely hurt and angry. A *panchayat* meeting was arranged and it culminated in a *talaaq*. Abbu snatched the six-month-old baby girl from his own daughter's bosom and handed her to the man who had divorced Chaandni, saying—"Wait and see, I shall remarry Chaandni before you can marry again."

He fulfilled his stubborn resolve. A Chaandni who was driven crazy with the pain of separation from her baby, pleaded over and over again—"Please do not force me to marry again. I will take care of my expenses by weaving."

But her screams went unheard. Within six months her second *nikah* took place in the village of Raghunathpur.

Beaten by the thrashings of time, a fearful and timid Chaandni entered this new *sasural*. Her new husband was aware of her first marriage and daughter, but he strictly warned Chaandni that she would have to suffer severe consequences if she ever uttered the name of her daughter. Chaandni hid her sorrow over her daughter in her heart and sealed her lips. She was afraid—"If he also divorces me, where would I go?"

So she prepared herself to endure another set of ordeals in this new *sasural*.

The families of Garima, Sandhya, Shikha and Pallavi were economically more secure and resourceful than were Radha and Chaandni's parents. For this reason, the sorrows that fell into the laps of these four women comprised fewer pains of livelihood and hunger, and more aches of middle-class respectability and caste-based social status. The misery that Garima, Sandhya and Shikha suffered as daughters of widowed mothers were those in which the colours of their mothers' agonies and sufferings had also blended thoroughly.

On the one hand Garima desired to doll herself up and prayed every day for a handsome partner of her choice. On the other hand, seeing her mother weighed down by the pressures of her relatives made Garima feel that she had become an enormous burden for her family. Once Nani even commented scathingly: "Mohan [Garima's father] had his alcohol and took off, but he left us to deal with all the hazards." Because of her lack of access to cash, Garima's mother was not in a position to give a big dowry. So, Nana, Mausa, Maa and even Garima herself always wished for a match to be arranged soon so that all these worries would come to an end.

In the end, Mausa managed to arrange a match without dowry—the boy used to work in the Sitapur eye hospital. But four days before the *tilak* ceremony, Garima's relatives discovered that the boy's family were not *kuleen* Brahmins. So the wedding was called off. After this, Mausa fixed Garima up with the fourth son of one of his sisters who was married in the village of Sujanpur. Nana consented to this match rather unenthusiastically because that family was known for its quarrelsome behavior. Garima's prospective sister-in-law, in particular, was infamous for her fights. However, Masi and Mausa assured the family that the boy himself was very good-natured.

Garima knew, because of distant kinship with this family, that people in her natal village of Manoharpur looked down upon Sujanpur because of its acute poverty. She detested even the sound of the word, "Sujanpur." She felt that her dreams had been crushed. She was reminded of all those married girls who had to visit their *mayaka* to collect essential items such as soap, toothpaste and hair oil. They didn't even get decent clothes to wear. "I am also going to be like one of them," Garima thought.

Everyone who heard about the engagement said the same thing, "Oh my God! Sujanpur is full of hooligans. Why are you marrying off your girl so far away? She won't even get any *roti* to eat."

The bride's side promised ten *beegha* of land to the groom's family and the match was settled. Grain had to be sold for the engagement ceremony. Garima's family gave plenty of purchased goods at the *tilak* but the Saas was infuriated because there wasn't enough cash, and she made a point of harping on this for several years with taunts and anger.

But in Garima's own home this was the first wedding, so all the rituals were carried out with great enthusiasm. Her Maa's tears, however, started flowing on the day that Garima got engaged. Maa trembled at the thought of being separated from her daughter, whose companionship had seen her through so many torturous years.

The wedding took place. In the beginning, Garima was always fearful, partly because of the new environment and partly because her heart was always seized by the memories of the violence that her own father wreaked on her mother. Even if it was something as small as an accidental oversalting of the food, Garima nervously prepared herself for being slapped and screamed at. But no such thing ever happened. Compared to her *mayaka*, there were fewer restrictions in her *sasural*. *Purdah* was also less. But her husband's laziness prevented him from making a reliable earning. This also created conflicts between mother and son, in which the nasty name-calling by Garima's Saas was always targeted at Garima and her mother.

All this shook Garima. But she was always satisfied by the fact that her own relationship with her husband was very solid. "Happy in my happiness, and sad in my sorrow"—Garima was content to find such a partner. Now, her biggest wish was that "Even if I have to lose everything I own, I pray that I never have to lose this relationship."

As we started looking for words to say and share the things that hid in our hearts with respect to love, we felt that it is easier to find happiness in a relationship as long as one does not have many expectations from it. When we begin to expect things from love, the search as well as the misery often intensify. Perhaps this was the reason why Pallavi, who was wedded in the Kumharawan village, continued to look for love several years after her marriage.

The man who was initially selected for Pallavi was a widower and a father of two. There was no demand for dowry. Pallavi thought she would be satisfied at least by the receipt of clothes and jewellery. But when she saw the photo of the prospective groom, it reminded her of her father. When the man came to see Pallavi, he himself said: "She is of the same age as my daughter. How can I accept her as my wife?"

Thank goodness that he refused this proposal himself, otherwise no one would have listened to Pallavi. But his refusal became a source of intense gossip and discussion in the village. People instantly blamed Pallavi's character; they said, "How can anyone reject such a beautiful girl? There must be something wrong with her."

Now what else can one call this besides vulgar abuse that even when a man of Pallavi's father's age thoughtfully declines the offer to marry an underage girl, the society condemns the girl? It is hardly surprising, then, that hundreds of accusations and questions continued to hound Pallavi for years after her marriage.

After this incident, Pallavi's marriage was arranged in Unnao district. The wedding invitations had been sent out, but at the time of the *tilak* there was a lot of bickering with respect to the exchange of gifts. The groom's side wanted ten thousand rupees. When they did not get so much, they came down to insulting Pallavi's family. Pallavi's Bhaiyya and Jijaji also refused to bend. The issue blew up. Pallavi's *tilak* was returned.

Now what could be more insulting than a daughter's tilak being returned from the *sasural*? The marriage was to take place in eight days. Amma and Babu wept: What would happen now? Where would they marry her now? Didi's Sasur tried to arrange a match with his good-for-nothing son, but thankfully Didi and Jijaji intervened and saved Pallavi. The home was drowned in an aura of mourning.

Babu was extremely disturbed. He left the house with Bhaiyya and Didi's Sasur, vowing that he would only return with a successful *tilak* accomplished. In a flash, Pallavi's marriage was arranged in the Kumharawan village, and this *tilak* was performed within three days of the unsuccessful *tilak* ceremony. The wedding was to take place in six days.

Right away, the groom's side made things clear—"We cannot get clothes or jewellery made for the Bahu on such a short notice. The wedding will take place with just one cotton *sari* and one nose ring, That's all."

Initially, there was no specific demand for dowry but during the *Kaleva* ceremony, that demand was also made. As soon as Pallavi arrived at the doorstep of her *sasural*, she heard her Saas remark, "They had come to arrange the wedding as if they were kings. But they didn't give us a damn thing!"

Pallavi's Saas took her straight to a store room in the house, half of which was filled with cow dung cakes and the other half with hay. Pallavi was instructed to sit on a *dari* on the hay. When she lifted her *ghoonghat*, she saw trash and cobwebs everywhere. She had seen dreams of a little room in her *sasural* in which she would sit and talk with her groom. But here she was, in this filthy little store room. She was so repulsed by this house that she could not eat or drink anything that day. She just lay down on the hay and slept. At night, when her groom entered the room, he first asked her name. Then he immediately queried, "What about your marriage in Jahanganj. Why did it not work out?"

Pallavi replied, "What do I know?"

Sleeping with a stranger on the first night of marriage was very difficult for Pallavi. She wept thinking that this is what she would have to undergo every day. The next day, she returned to her *mayaka* with her husband for a total of one day, and then came back to her *sasural*.

Pallavi had her period before marriage but none afterwards. The midwife announced that she was pregnant. The Saas suspected that the pregnancy happened before marriage; that's why the girl was married off in such haste. Pallavi refused to provide any explanations. Two and a half months went by. Then she returned to her *mayaka*.

Pallavi had difficulty appearing in her *mayaka* with an expanding belly. After spending three months there, she wrote to her husband asking him to take her back home. But it was her Sasur who came to fetch her. Amma served him *daal*, rice, *roti* and *sabzi*. Sasur ate everything there, but as soon as he arrived in the *sasural*, he announced before half the village: "The first thing those rascals fed me was *daal* and rice. They are worthless. They should have at least fed *poori* and *sabzi* to a guest on the first day! It is a women's kingdom there—there is no *purdah*, no nothing. Samdhin (Pallavi's mother) was staring at me naked-faced, shamelessly asking me how I was doing!"

Even after suffering all this abuse, Pallavi eagerly awaited her reunion with her husband. But something vicious must have happened while she was gone, because her husband completely stopped coming near her. He would not even ask how she was doing. When he came home for lunch, Pallavi had to remain in the *ghoonghat* because of family pressure. When he came at other times, the young Nanads (sisters-in-law) did not leave them alone. There was no place or opportunity for a conversation or intimacy of any kind.

Pallavi became restless. Then she had a brain wave—"My husband grinds the fodder every afternoon. If I start operating the machine, at least I would be able to see him to my heart's content. At least, I will be able to touch his hands."

But what happened was exactly the opposite. Her husband instructed his brother to assist Pallavi with the fodder processing, and he himself sat outside until the processor was turned off. Pallavi cursed her parents as she ground the fodder—"Rather than subjecting me to a life like this, it would have been better if they had fed me Sulfas" (chemical fertilizer)!

When Pallavi could no longer bear this rejection, she forced her husband to come close to her. She conceived a second time and gave birth to a daughter. The husband's distant attitude continued until the birth of their third child.

Today, Pallavi wonders why life played such a harsh joke on her. So intense is this nameless pain that the society does not even allow a woman to express it to anyone. After all, who will understand the emptiness that ripped Pallavi's insides for so many years? People would simply say that if her husband didn't love her, how could she have three children. But is love merely about having sex? Doesn't emotional or psychological intimacy matter in a relationship between a woman and man? Pallavi keeps searching for an answer to the question of why she remained so unsatisfied for years, even after becoming a mother of three children.

Shikha's mother also started worrying prematurely about shipping off her daughter to her "own home." It had been three years since she had lost her husband, and Shikha was now completing her fifteenth year. The older sister mentioned a possible match in Chandosi village. When mother went to check him out, she found that he was the oldest son in his family with four younger brothers and sisters. All the younger siblings were aged between seven years and nine months. When she returned she told Shikha that the family was fine and the boy worked in a shop.

The boy's horoscope was requested. In response, however, no horoscope was delivered; only the warning that it was a large household and there would be plenty of work. Somehow, mother managed to arrange some money and jewellery and Shikha was married off.

Shikha had to cook *rotis* for the afternoon meal even on the day the wedding procession was to arrive. Her mother kept moaning and groaning that her daughter could not get a bit of rest on the day of her own wedding. Shikha was fearful of what was coming next. She wondered whether the beatings would resume as soon as she reached *sasural*. Tears choked her as she thought of going so far away from her mother, brothers and sisters.

On the night after the wedding, Shikha was to meet her husband for the first time. She was led into a room where many items from the family shop were stuffed in gunnysacks. There, her husband was sleeping on a cot. Exhausted, Shikha also lay down on a flattened gunnysack and went to sleep. Suddenly, when her husband's sleep was interrupted by something, he rose up and took Shikha to his bed. Before making love, he told her many things about his family and household. He instructed her about how she was to behave with him in his home and society.

Other members of the household did not stay too far behind in giving directives: Shikha was ordered to touch everyone's feet and bend her head when she sat down. She had to speak softly, and cook the meals only after checking the menu with everyone. She had to do all the big and small chores around the house. And every night, she had to press her mother-in-law's legs and seek her permission before going to bed. So many instructions were bombarded at Shikha as soon as she entered a new house! She began to panic.

In spite of a house full of people, Shikha felt lonely in her *sasural*. Her husband loathed having conversations about everyday household matters. His family was somewhat anti-social; the only people who visited were close relatives. Shikha kept busy with domestic chores all day, and listened to the incessant grumbles and complaints of her Saas and older Nanad. Her five-year-old sister-in-law, Neetu, was Shikha's only soul-mate. Whenever Shikha became troubled or exhausted, she sent Neetu off with some money to buy a postcard and wrote a letter home. In her letters, she often pleaded her mother to send someone back to fetch her. Maa would send Mausia to bring her back for fifteen days, but on the fifteenth day someone from the *sasural* appeared at the doorstep to bring her back. On her way back from her *mayaka*, Shikha was imprisoned again as soon as she crossed the intersection of Chandosi. Her husband would remark, "Cover yourself, or someone will see you with an exposed face." She had to comply by pulling over a *ghoonghat*. And no ordinary *ghoonghat* at that—it had be as long as an arm with a *chadar* thrown on top!

Many times Shikha felt saddened by the distance between her dreams and the reality she faced. Even so, she accepted whatever she got and sealed her lips. Ever since she started figuring out the world, there was one thing that she had clearly understood: If there are any women who are considered worthy, civilized and respectable in the world, it is those who learn to suppress their own desires.

On the surface, Shikha's story might seem simpler than the stories of the other six diary writers, because she faced fewer material deprivations and hardships. Shikha cannot claim in any way that she was living on the margins of her society. But what she experienced more than anyone else was the weight of the norms, regulations and hollow values of middle class society. The burden of so-called respectability and honour and the endless pressure of keeping everything hidden that crushed Shikha in her *mayaka* now started following her in her *sasural* in a more ferocious form.

The Joys and Sorrows of Motherhood

In my *sasural*, Tau's wife once gave birth to a boy. Upset with her for some reason, her Saas stirred poison in her teacup. The Bahu died. Without fuss, her mother made a deal with the Saas and gave the

> new-born for adoption... People consider it a good omen when a woman dies before her husband. I was often grabbed by the idea...of killing myself. But each time, the love of my daughter stopped me. What would my daughter do if I were gone?
>
> —From Madhulika's diary

> My Saas gave birth to a daughter after my marriage. Standing in the middle of the courtyard, my Sasur uttered some foul words and ordered her, "Come on, wench. Attend to the cow now. Or are you waiting for your father to bring the milk to feed your girl?" I felt awful. I thought, 'When I gave birth to my son it was hours before the cord was cut. What would happen at the birth of this girl?'
>
> —From Pallavi's diary

We had heard so much for so long about becoming a mother. Motherhood arrived as a very critical and important event in all our lives, but in so many different forms and ways. While the long absence of a child brought happiness in some cases, her birth caused disaster in others. Our diverse circumstances continued to knit and weave our joys of motherhood in varied shapes and definitions.

Within ten months of marriage, a fifteen-year-old Pallavi became the mother of a son. Pallavi was cooking when her labour pains gained full force. There was no one around to help. The boy was born in the kitchen. The village women rushed over as soon as the news spread, and as they arrived each of them began by counting how many months had passed since her marriage.

It began to dawn on Pallavi that not a single one of them cared about the fact that she had become a mother, or about the difficulty she had endured while giving birth alone. Most significant was the gossip about whether or not the child was conceived before marriage. Perhaps people were more inclined to suspect this because Pallavi was a beautiful and educated young woman raised in the town, and her husband was exactly her opposite in every way. Everyone suspected that she must have carried a "gift" in her womb; why else were her parents so quick to fix her up with a worthless man?

It was wintertime. The son was born at approximately seven in the morning, and the Dhankun arrived at two in the afternoon to cut the umbilical cord. Until then, Pallavi and her newborn just lay around waiting. Saas said that a newborn can only wear the new clothes that come from the *mayaka*. Thus, the child got new clothes at the age of three months when Pallavi's mother managed to send some over. Saas used to sit around all day with the newborn in her lap so that Pallavi would have to run about and do all the household chores. When it was time to nurse the baby, he was placed in Pallavi's arms and then taken away again. The child was well looked after because he was a boy, but no one cared about Pallavi. Thank goodness this first child was a son. If he had been born a girl, Pallavi's life would have been an endless misery.

A daughter and another son were born after this one. On the one hand, there was the constant distance from her husband, and on the other hand, there was the birth of these three children in quick succession. Pallavi's heart was always torn apart by the thought, "Oh my God, what kind of a relationship is this?" This heartache constantly pricked the corners of her eyes in the form of unwept tears.

If the world could not accept the fact of Pallavi's early motherhood, it also could not spare Radha for remaining childless for three years after marriage. All the time she heard only one complaint, "Oh, it seems that she is infertile!"

The women of the extended family always taunted, "She is educated. We can bet you that she eats something to prevent pregnancy!"

When Radha finally conceived, she didn't get enough to eat or drink. Because of weakness, the labour lasted for four painful days. She gave birth to a son. When he was barely one month old, Saas and Radha had a big quarrel. Later, Sasur and Saas threw all of Radha's belongings outside the house and took away all the jewellery that they had given her. After having a grandson, Radha's Saas was confident that no matter how much she tortured Radha, she wouldn't leave. After she became a mother, there was hardly any risk of Radha remarrying into another family.

A second son was born three years after the first one. When Radha discovered that she was pregnant, her husband threatened that she would be responsible for the consequences if she gave birth to a girl. This threat pierced Radha's heart like a thorn. She left for her *mayaka* two months before the baby was due. She stayed there until her second son was born.

When her second born was just an infant, Radha got employment in NSY. As the pressure of the new job mounted, all the responsibility of the newborn fell on her husband. Radha had no time to attend to the children. The little boy became sick, and even before the doctors could detect what was ailing him, this little piece of Radha's heart passed away.

This tragedy jolted her husband. It became unbearable for him to accept the death of a son for whom he had done everything. For Radha, this death brought many traumas—first she had to bear the sorrow of losing her child, then it was her husband's illness and deep depression, and on top of that she was tormented by profound guilt. She was convinced that if she had not been too preoccupied with work to take care of her child, none of them would have to bear such a huge mountain of sorrow...

Radha gave birth to another son exactly nine months after the death of her second born.

When a thirteen-year-old Chaandni got married, she was a child in age as well as in body. She started menstruating when she lost her virginity after the wedding. Just two months later, she conceived her first child. Chaandni was deeply disappointed when she found out that she was pregnant. But this was only the beginning of many disappointments.

The ordeals piled on with the birth of the daughter. Chaandni and her newborn were completely ignored. Then, within six months, the daughter was snatched away from her before the eyes of the entire village. With the pain of this profound loss hidden in her chest, Chaandni once again became pregnant in Raghunathpur village after her second marriage. Here, Chaandni was absolutely alone when she had her first son. There were two Muslim midwives in the village but neither could make it when Chaandni was in labour. One was ill and the other one had gone out of the village. Her husband was forced to go to the home of a midwife from the Maurya caste and ask for assistance. But the Maurya midwife flatly refused to extend a hand for this work in a Muslim home.

The son's birth was like a balm to Chaandni's wounded heart that was still mourning the separation from her first daughter. But there was no respite from the quarrels at home. At times, Chaandni felt like poisoning herself and putting an end to her daily misery. But gradually, she accumulated the strength to endure with the emotional support of her son. As she struggled on, two more daughters were born.

Her husband declared after the birth of his second daughter that he no longer wanted to live with Chaandni. He was sickened that Chaandni went on producing more and more daughters! Within five days of giving birth to her second daughter, all the familial responsibilities in and out of the home fell on Chaandni. With wet eyes and a sore body, Chaandni recalled the torture that her own Amma went through when she sat at the loom immediately after Chaandni's birth. Chaandni does not know exactly why, but somehow she felt her own pain lessen every time she remembered Amma's pain.

Chaandni had another son but he could not stand up even after he was five. It was not polio. That much Chaandni knew. But no one could figure out what was eating this child. Sixteen thousand rupees were spent on his treatment, but with no luck. The little one probably figured out that he was going very far, very soon. So as he was dying, he requested his mother—"Ammi, will you let me have your milk one more time?"

Chaandni was shocked by his pleading. She was nursing an infant daughter at the time, but how could she find the heart to say no to this dying son? But the poor thing did not even have the energy to drink her milk. He was gone as soon as Chaandni pulled him close to her breast.

But how strange are these associations of heart, soul and body! Chaandni gave birth to a son ten months after the death of this child, in the same way that Radha found another son after the loss of one.

Sandhya did not think it was a good idea to have a baby soon after marriage. What would people say? She had always heard from the old women in the villages that a newly wedded girl should eat, play and laugh a lot during the first four-five years of marriage.

Only after that should she embark on motherhood. This belief prevented Sandhya from wanting a baby even three years after her marriage. While Radha was subjected to scornful meddling for not producing a child after three years of marriage, here was Sandhya, feeling a different kind of pressure: not to have one.

Sandhya had not even completed the first trimester of her pregnancy when she dislocated her right hip. When the pain increased, she became bed-ridden. But the pressure of household chores did not let up. Sandhya figured that no one would expect her to work if she stopped eating. For two days she didn't eat or work. But on the third day, her sister-in-law announced, "Eating or not eating is up to you. But as long as you are living in the *sasural*, you will have to do your share of work."

Sandhya's pregnancy related ailments continued to worsen. Her husband also wanted her to escape from his home and get some rest in her *mayaka*, but he was too hesitant to express any of this before his own relatives. Eventually, Sandhya herself sent for her relatives with the news about her illness. Her brother came to fetch her. It was in her *mayaka*, then, that her first son was born.

When Garima did not give birth even after three years of marriage, people started worrying. She was medically treated for infertility. She finally conceived after five years of marriage. During the pregnancy, Garima was nicely pampered. Her Saas, Devar, Nanad and husband all took good care of her. Garima was fed a lot of milk, ghee and coconut so that the newborn would come out strong and light complexioned.

At the time of the labour, however, the baby ended up in a dangerous position. Because her *sasural* was far away from the town of Unnao, Garima could not be taken to the hospital in time. The baby boy died in birth. For Garima this loss of her first child was unbearable.

The loss overwhelmed Garima once again when she was giving birth to her daughter after some time. Her heartache was particularly acute when she noticed her mother-in-law's enthusiasm vanishing upon seeing that the newborn was a girl.

But her husband reassured her by saying that this second daughter was far better than the first son. At least the little girl did not throw the family into mourning at the time of birth.

When Madhulika became pregnant for the first time, sometimes she was deprived of food, and sometimes of cover. The first conception happened two and a half years after marriage, but the girl died inside the womb before she was born. If Madhulika had reached the hospital in time, the baby could have been saved.

After this, Madhulika gave birth to another daughter. Fortunately, her Nanad was also pregnant at the same time, so Madhulika also got a share of some of the attention and care that her sister-in-law was getting.

Six years after her daughter's birth, Madhulika had a son. Delivered by the experienced hands of Chaandni in January 2003 during the first discussion session of our diaries, this new son was collectively named Sarthak, or meaningful, by the nine *sangtins* on this journey.

Questions Within Questions

After writing down all these intimate moments and events that marked our long journey from adolescence to motherhood, we feel overwhelmed and drained. We are also gripped by an obvious question: What are we trying to tell you—our readers—by engaging in this exercise of writing? Are these stories important simply because they were articulated as a result of a collective process? Or, are we trying to share something new or unique with you through these stories?

In reality, we know full weli that there is nothing new in our stories. In fact, in many places our lives are entangled in precisely the same webs of events and complications as those our mothers, aunts, sisters, sisters-in-law and neighbourhood women find themselves trapped in day and night. There is no doubt that the process of collectively writing, sharing and reflecting upon these very ordinary experiences of our everyday lives has given us new eyes to understand several aspects of our society—whether it is the relationships between women and men, or the various reasons behind women's oppression, or even the fissures that exist among castes, classes and rural-urban locations. When these issues are raised within government and voluntary organizations, however, they are often split into specialized topics rather than being tackled as interconnected. For this reason our analysis, and our struggles, remain at times incomplete, at times hollow. Through this collective process we have tried to step out of this hollowness and incompleteness to understand our social complexities a little closer-up, a little deeper-down.

One question that emerged in relation to our diaries and which took us by surprise pertained to moments of happiness. It is not as if we never encountered any happy moments while living in our *sasurals*. Then why did such moments remain almost entirely unwritten in our diaries?

Some of us thought that perhaps there would have been less sadness and more joy if more of us had married men of our own choice. But then we wonder whether that is really accurate. Let us take Radha, for instance. She got the chance to marry a man of her choice, but was she able to protect herself from the everyday restrictions, humiliations and battery? In fact, it became even more challenging for Radha to bear these because she could not openly share her difficulties with anyone. Whenever she tried, people said—"What can we do? Didn't you choose him?"

Should we then conclude that the wounds of sorrows resided so deep in our heads and hearts that the faint marks of happiness just faded away? Or else, is it possible that we got so entwined in the grief of not realizing our dreams that we failed to identify the flashes of happiness when they came our way. And those happy moments slipped out of our hands before we could seize them?

The biggest burden that we have carried since the onset of our youth until this day is the weight of the so-called respectability of our families, clans and relatives. The definitions of caste and familial honour that were imposed upon us in the name of this respectability at times included demands for dowry, at times strict *purdah* and at others, sheer slavery. To save the *naak* (honour) of our husbands, fathers-in-law, fathers and brothers, sometimes our *tilak* was returned and at others we were forcibly married. Sometimes, the loyalty of our wombs was questioned, and at others our nursing infant was forcibly snatched from us and given away.

If seen in totality, our experiences resonate with what Radha once wrote in her diary—that the rules and regulations associated with youth and marriage ensure that our entire being and existence become someone else's possessions. For example, whether a strict *purdah* is slapped upon us in the name of religion or respectability, its objective is always to guarantee that a woman's freedom remains at the mercy of her husband and *sasural*. But even when a woman is outside of the *purdah*, her body and sexuality are still considered to be the property of her husband. Whenever the husband wants, he can become sexually intimate with his wife; and whenever he pleases, he can discard her physically and emotionally to weep tears of helplessness and frustration.

And the inconsistencies do not end here. On the axis of the same so-called respectability spin all those definitions of masculinity, the burden which our men and society carry out so faithfully and laboriously. Shouldering the traditional burden of masculinity, the world sometimes asks Pallavi the reasons behind her broken marriage and inquires about the paternity of her first offspring. And sometimes it insists on erasing the faintest trace of Chaandni's tiny daughter, so that no one can find out that Chaandni had been "owned" by another man before her current husband. Today, Chaandni's first daughter is married, but for seventeen years Chaandni did not even utter this daughter's name. When in December 2002, during the process of collective diary writing, Chaandni shared the pain of her separation from her daughter for the first time, we were shaken. Our hearts were tormented by a thousand questions: Why did Chaandni and her daughter have to suffer this enormous pain? Why is it so hard for Chaandni's husband to accept the reality of her first marriage even to this day? Why did Chaandni have to deny the existence of her previous husband and offspring in order to obtain a second husband? All of this makes us wonder about the fragility of the masculinity that our society nurtures and worships night and day. It starts cracking with the slightest scratch on patriarchy!

And there is no respite from these pretenses and humiliations of *izzat*, *aabroo* and masculinity even when the husband dies.

A woman without a husband is first made dependent on all the men in her *sasural* and *mayaka*. And then, labeling the same women as a bad omen, the society cruelly forces her to the sidelines so that she is denied the right to participate in the joys of her own children, into the raising of whom she has poured her entire being. Is this not an accurate description of what happened with Sandhya's and Garima's mother? Both widowed women were kept away from the rituals of their own daughters' weddings because they were regarded as inauspicious. All the ceremonies associated with Garima's wedding were performed by her Tauji and Taiji. When Tauji started performing *Dwarchar*, Garima's mother fainted. Seeing her mother's condition, Garima began to cry. She could not understand at that time who should be blamed for her mother's situation: Garima herself? Or all those values, rules and regulations that forcibly snatch away all the support systems from a "manless" woman? At the time Garima's hand was placed in her husband's hand in matrimony, she was overcome with pain, thinking: "Now, I am married. I have no choice. Rather than being separated from my mother, it would be better to die this instant."

When Sandhya saw her brothers worry about her marriage, she also wished that she were dead. At the time when Sandhya's wedding ceremony was being performed, the sorrow of losing her husband became a fresh wound for Sandhya's mother. It is amazing to think how big a role rituals play in ripening and reviving women's sorrows.

As we narrated and braided together these moments of our lives, we were struck by how the beliefs and dreams that we inherited from our society since early childhood had unknowingly become so heavy. In our dreams, there was neither any respect for the dark skin, nor for the rural lives of peasants or labourers. We also felt that compared to our childhood, issues of caste and class became hazier in the writing of our marriages and motherhoods. It was primarily the making and breaking of our relationships with *mayaka* and *sasural*, and the many expectations and responsibilities associated with these places, that continued to weigh on our minds and hearts.

Despite this, the inequalities of caste and class emerged with sharp edges several times, which kept reminding us of the ways in which the structures of caste difference drape different kinds of uniforms on the burdens of *izzat* and *aabroo*. For example, when Garima reached puberty, her mother worried that one wrong step by her daughter would bring disgrace to the honour of her Brahmin clan. In contrast, Radha's parents, who were fighting with poverty and untouchability, found themselves under a double burden. Their hearts were wrapped in the fear that if any Sawarn man made sexual advances towards their daughter, the family would have no place to hide.

Similarly, when Pallavi was alone at the time of her first labour, she went through the pain of not having anyone to turn to at this difficult time. But she didn't have to suffer the humiliation associated with untouchability that Chaandni had to suffer in her second *sasural* because of the attitude of the Maurya midwives. This insult hurt Chaandni so much that she vowed to become a midwife. And since she has learned this work, no power in the world has been able to place a shadow of untouchability or discrimination on her work. No matter who needs her and where, Chaandni makes it a point to reach her at any cost.

In the same way, many aspects of domestic and familial violence also get trapped in the swamps of casteism, wealth and poverty. When the policies of the government continuously disempower the poor and Dalit both economically and socially, and when gambling and alcohol emerge as new symbols of masculinity in this context, then, in the midst of these worsening conditions, where can women like Madhulika, Radha and Chaandni turn to look for a ray of hope?

As we listened to each other's stories of adolescence, marriage and *sasural*, we found our circumstances, worries and oppressions hovering around the things done to us by our own mothers, mothers-in-law or sisters-in-law. Eventually, when we sat down to analyse this, we were confronted by the question, what do we want to gain by telling these stories? Are we not trying to verify the same old saying that a woman is a woman's worst enemy?

Absolutely not. We feel that such sayings do no justice to the complexities of women's lives.

Garima thinks that her mother wanted to beat her into becoming so "civilized" and subservient that she would never have to be scorned or insulted in her *sasural*. Similarly, the mothers of Pallavi and Madhulika believed that if their *bitiyas* were made accustomed to an array of pressures, controls and insults in their *mayakas*, they would be able to live through any calamity in their *sasurals* with great ease. Sometimes, the bone-breaking beatings and scoldings of their Ammas got so thoroughly mingled with their own tears and love that it became impossible to separate the two.

Upon coming to the *sasural*, our relationships with our mothers-in-law remained similarly wrapped in multiple layers. In our *mayakas*, we had often noticed that instead of scolding us directly, our fathers terrorized us by petrifying our mothers. Similarly, the responsibility of saving the *izzat* of the men in our *sasural* fell on our mothers- and sisters-in-law. Moreover, how can we deny the privileges that are bestowed upon a woman in our patriarchal system with the arrival of mother-in-lawhood? After years of being crushed as daughters-in-law in the grinding mill of the *sasural*, how can mothers-in-law overcome the temptation of enjoying the benefits of their newly acquired power? As long as our structures of family and marriage remain the same, it would be impossible for our mothers-in-law to resist this temptation.

In the end, a few words about those silences and whispers that we could not stop from penetrating our writing despite the many vows of openness, honesty and confidentiality that we had all taken. Approximately two months after the writing and collective discussions of our diaries, when we sat down to discuss the outline of this book, the issue of *samlaingikta* (same-sex sexuality) arose for the first time in our discussions. We often feel that the manner in which this topic is commonly addressed in our trainings or meetings gives women from our environment very few tools to engage or connect with it.

Out of all the diary writers, it was only Radha who was able to muster the courage to share an incident that had taken place with her best friend, even though most of us admitted, without offering any specifics, that we had encountered such intimacies in our lives in one form or another. Despite our common experiences, this conversation about *samlaingikta* was not so easy for us. But when we started to discuss this we were pulled deeper and deeper into its complexities, especially when Pallavi directly connected the complexities of love and sexuality with the struggle of her own life. What kinds of physical, mental and emotional relationships are possible for us to create between women and men in this world of ours? And which are all those relationships that we desperately wished for but could never build with our husbands? What about the intimacies that we could never live inspite of dreaming endlessly about them? How did our familial structures and processes of socialization prevent us from developing these relationships? If they so desire, why can't women come together to create all those intimacies that they can often never live or find with men in our society? As we spun in this cycle of questions, we learned for the first time to recognize and make space for *samlaingikta*, not as a light subject that was a world apart from our own lives and sufferings, but as a critical social issue.

There were other junctures as well when some voices remained quiet. We felt that Chaandni had managed to open the box in her chest; several others thrashed about trying to open their own hidden boxes, but their lids still remained half-shut. Perhaps it would not be wrong to say that Chaandni was able to muster the courage to open the box that had remained closed for seventeen years, for the simple reason that her first child was born inside wedlock. If this daughter had come into her life out of wedlock, could she have shared so quickly this pain that she had guarded so earnestly for so many years?

So, as we end the story of our long journey from the threshold of adolescence to the doorstep of motherhood, our only wish is to find the strength to end the restlessness caused by the half-shut boxes that are still hiding in our chests... And along with the sharpening of our analytical abilities, we wish to open the doors of others' hearts in such a way that we can all find enough space to fight our battles against everyday social, physical and emotional exploitation, and so that the voices that have been suffocating for years can find the desired notes to sing and scream.

Notes

[1] Opening line of a famous folk song from rural Uttar Pradesh.

Prisons Within Prisons: Battles Stretching from the Courtyard to the Mind

> In my home, when [people] discovered that I was going to take up a job, my Sasurji began to scream, "If my Bahu works outside the house, I will hang myself. I have so much. A woman from my house does not need to work outside." My husband was also angry. .[He] declared one day: "..Do whatever you want. It's up to you to either keep our honour, or to raze it." I began to think—Which honour do these people keep invoking, after all? Where does this mighty honour disappear when my son lives in my *mayaka* and my mother bears all his expenses? When I live without soap or oil, then the honour stays alive but when I talk about earning two pennies, that same honour makes its way to the coffin!
>
> — From Pallavi's diary

Leaping across the boundaries of our homes was not easy for any of us. Our different circumstances and home environments translated into different kinds of risks and battles for each of us as we stepped into our work-field. And once we entered it, so completely were we consumed by our work that the current of our life changed forever. There was a time when we did not even have the confidence that we could get an ordinary job in a government-run women's programme. But very soon there came a time when, immersed in our work, we had travelled so far that the significance of a "job" began to fade from our minds. Every pore in our body was now intoxicated with the desire to change our society.

This journey of mind-sets, ideologies and struggles shook our personal and collective lives and relationships. We resolved to fulfill our crushed dreams and to claim back the rights that were snatched away from us. As we battled for our rights to earn our livelihoods, to educate ourselves, and to define our own freedom—we were forced to listen to our own voices and interrogate our inherited definitions of stigma, infamy and familial values. Our inner confidence and courage swelled in direct proportion to the number of boundaries we crossed and the oppositions that came our way.

With this, we also started the process of identifying the mental and social swamps that mired our experiences, our social and religious beliefs and our values. Despite our countless attempts, we could neither begin to bridge the yawning gulfs that surrounded us, nor could we rid them of the poison that was planted deep inside them. To tell the truth, it was only when we wrote and shared our diaries that we could begin to untie by ourselves—and with each other—the tight knots of poison that were implanted within the many layers of our hearts.

In this chapter, we give words to the fragments of these entangled stories related to our work lives—how we stepped out of our homes and became involved with our work on women's issues, the kinds of dilemmas and inner battles we faced during the process of joining our work, and how the paths that we chose gave us new insights to see and assess the inequalities of caste, religion and class that resided so deeply in our society.

Arrival of Feminism in a Swamp of Casteism and Classism

In 1996, NSY started finding its feet in Sitapur under the leadership of Richa Singh. The launching of the programme was accompanied by a search for village-level workers who could mobilize the poorest and Dalit rural women in the "field." These mobilizers or field activists were sought from the same villages in which the work of women's empowerment was to occur, so that together they could raise women's issues, give birth to women's collectives in the villages, and take their collective understanding to the next stage.

Out of the seven diary writers, Madhulika, Shikha and Pallavi were selected in August 1996 as field-level workers. Although Sandhya was also in the same pool of applicants, she was selected to run a literacy centre in the first phase of NSY's work. It was only after serving as a teacher in a literacy centre for a year and a half that she assumed the responsibility of a field-level worker. Similarly, Garima first joined NSY as an office worker on daily wages. She wanted to get a permanent placement as a member of the office staff, but when she was not chosen for such a position in an informal selection process, she was forced to accept the job of a field-level worker. Radha joined as a field-level worker in 1998, and later, it was through Radha that Chaandni entered the organization as a teacher in a literacy centre.

The news that workers were being sought to build grassroots women's collectives reached the seven autobiographers in different circumstances and through different channels of information. Fighting with her own doubts and fears, each one amassed the nerve to take the next step.

Radha writes, "I had a really hard time meeting my daily expenses. I used to stay depressed, thinking, 'how long will things go on like this?' I was prepared to work outside the home but my husband did not agree. Defeated, I had to sit at home...Here in [NSY], they were looking for another fieldworker. Didi [Richa Singh] came to my house to talk with me and my husband about this. His disapproval persisted. But after talking to Didi, I felt so confident that I stepped out to work despite my husband's opposition."

Madhulika, who was working as a volunteer in Manpur village, was similarly approached by the district-level team of NSY. When Madhulika got ready to go to the district office of NSY for the first time, no one from her family was willing to accompany her. This hostility hurt Madhulika. She cried a lot. Eventually, her husband and sister-in-law agreed to come to town with her. If there was a dream that Madhulika had nurtured since she was very little, it was the dream of having a salaried job! But as they approached the office, Madhulika, an eighth grade graduate, was seized by worries: What sort of people would greet me there? I have such little education. Why on earth would anyone want to give me a job there?

For Pallavi, Sandhya, Garima, Shikha and Chaandni, their first introduction to NSY happened rather differently. The information that NSY was looking for field-level workers reached Pallavi through her older sister Sunita, who worked in another local NGO. The same Sunita also carried this good news to their relative, Shikha. In Sahjanpur village, Sandhya's widowed neighbour, Jamuna, had to give up her newly-found job in NSY due to familial pressures. She told Sandhya, "I am not going to be able to continue my job. If you are interested in it, you should apply for the same job."

Sandhya and Garima were both going through economic crises in their families. Hence, Sandhya's sister-in-law, Kiran, who was employed as a teacher in a primary school, advised both of them to try to find a place in NSY. Chaandni's story has an entirely different trajectory from the rest. She was introduced to NSY through Radha at a time when Chaandni discovered that Radha was looking for someone to run a literacy centre in Jagrauli, one of the villages in Radha's *field*.

In this story of how the seven autobiographers were introduced to NSY, it is noteworthy that the two Dalit workers—Radha and Madhulika—were the only ones to be approached by the organization during the initial phase of 1996-1998. All the workers from the Sawarn castes—Pallavi, Shikha, Sandhya and Garima—received the information about the organization through their own personal channels. There is no doubt that the organization had earned the reputation of working among Dalit and oppressed women, and it had also consciously tried to seek workers from the same groups. Yet, despite sincere efforts to employ workers from Dalit castes, only two workers came from this category. Of these, too, Madhulika came in 1996 and Radha was not able to join until 1998. Chaandni joined even later directly through Radha's intervention. In this little story of the crossing and passing of information about job vacancies, it is impossible to overlook how news related to new opportunities travels fastest to those groups and castes who already have greater access to, and control over, resources. Certainly, NSY was looking for field-level workers at that time, and these four women from upper castes were facing tough economic circumstances; all four were quite eager to earn a living that would allow them to improve the material conditions of their lives.

In the end, events took such a course that all of them joined NSY.

And Thus We Stepped Out of Our Cages

All of us had long harboured the desire of working outside our homes. Opportunities also came our way, but so did countless hurdles!

The first step in the journey was to wrench ourselves out of the worry that no one would give jobs to poor or less educated women like us. When we untangled ourselves from this fear, the opposition of our family members was waiting to greet us. In every home, the same logic was used to deter us: "What will people say if you start working outside?"

Notwithstanding the enormous distances of caste and religion that separated us, several of us faced similar strictness of *purdah* in our homes—even if the reasons behind the restrictions varied radically. For Chaandni, it was impossible to even imagine that she would get her family's permission to run a literacy centre in another village. First, it involved working with Hindus day and night. Second, she would have to travel alone for miles every day.

Burdened by the hollow values of upper caste respectability and familial honour, Shikha was cooped up in such a cursed cage that she could not even open the windows in her home to look outside. Although her family was more prosperous than the other six, the *purdah* that she faced was also the most restrictive. She had to maintain *purdah* even in front of the domestic workers in her *sasural*. This enabled the members of her *sasural* to boast proudly that no one could even get a glimpse of their Bahu's face! Such traps of respectability and honour continued to stifle Shikha for ten years after her marriage, even when she became a mother of three. We can only imagine how challenging her struggle to break those prison walls must have been.

In our villages, the upper caste folks often mock the *purdah* of the Dalits by saying: "Is their *purdah* any *purdah*? Today the *doli* has gone; tomorrow the bride is cutting grass in her rags!" In an ironic way, this proverb captures many realities; but it is hardly applicable in all situations. For one, it did not apply to Radha. The *purdah* in Radha's home was so strict that she wasn't even allowed to sit among women of her own extended family. Whenever anyone entered the house from the outside, she had to leave and hide herself inside. The cause of this *purdah*, however, was not a false show of respectability, but the fear in the hearts of Radha's parents-in-law that if Radha was not prevented from meeting other people, she might get tricked by others into leaving her *sasural* and return to her *mayaka*.

In such circumstances, obtaining the consent of our family members to work outside seemed like an impossible task to some of us. On top of that, women from our neighbourhoods were not making things any easier. They did not miss a single opportunity to sneer at us: "If our daughter-in-law had got out of control like this, we would have broken her limbs!"

Such comments served to add fuel to the fire. In Pallavi's home, her father-in-law got so enraged about the wounding of his family's honour that all hell broke loose. His wife supported him completely. A similar situation prevailed in Madhulika's home; her Devar, who was unemployed himself, could not digest the idea of his Bhabhi getting a job. When Madhulika returned home from her first official meeting, she was carrying a diary that she got from NSY. At that time, some of her Devar's money was kept in the house. When the Devar saw her diary, he assumed without asking that Madhulika had given away his money in a bribe to get a job. This misunderstanding exploded into a big fight. In the initial phase, when Madhulika had to travel to faraway villages for her work, her family members refused to support her at all.

Despite these familial restrictions and hostilities, it would be inaccurate to say that each one of us confronted similar kinds of opposition. Sandhya, Garima and Shikha faced far fewer restrictions from their husbands and considerably more support for outside employment than did Pallavi, Radha and Madhulika, whose husbands openly confronted them.

Chaandni's circumstances were relatively more complicated. From the very beginning, Chaandni had been in the habit of earning a small income through her weaving. She writes, "I used to get depressed when I didn't have any money in my own hands."

In Chaandni's *sasural*, the family relied on farming instead of weaving, and Chaandni was completely inexperienced in farm work. Once she got an offer to work as a helper in the Aanganwadi programme in her village. When she sought her husband's consent, she met an outright refusal: "I cannot tolerate the idea of you fetching kids from the homes of Chamars and Paasis [for the Aanganwaḍi]. If you managed to get a job in some kind of literacy centre, I wouldn't mind that."

The hardships at Chaandni's home continued to mount. At this time, Radha appeared like an angel in Chaandni's life. Radha was looking for a teacher to run a literacy centre in one of the villages of her *field*. When she chatted with Chaandni's husband, he immediately agreed, saying – "Go. If the job involves educating others, you must do it." Chaandni thinks that perhaps it was in the hope of proving something to the world that her husband consented to her employment; otherwise it would have been extremely tough for her to run a literacy centre in another village. Even with his permission, however, she was not spared from the derision of her husband and family members.

When we connect these politics with caste and religion, an interesting picture begins to emerge. Three out of these seven autobiographers—that is, Garima, Sandhya and Shikha—came from Sawarn families whose economic circumstances were less constrained than those of the others'. Far from deterring them from taking up employment, their family members broke their orthodox values and supported them when they saw a "respectable" job. However, Pallavi faced greater financial hardships than these three, despite being Sawarn. The opposition from her family members was also quite strong. One possible explanation for this is that Pallavi's family is surrounded by Brahmins on all sides, and members of her *sasural* always feel pressured to remain faithful to brahmanical beliefs and practices. In contrast, the opposition faced by Radha and Madhulika, who come from Dalit backgrounds, and by Chaandni, who comes from a Sunni Muslim family, was partly due to the desire of their family members to keep their daughters-in-law locked inside the homes in the name of respectability so that nobody from the upper tiers of the village community could point fingers at them.

It might seem strange, but the reality is that the majority of women in our writing collective continued to abide by the rules of *purdah* to some degree or another, even after becoming NGO-workers. In fact, their work forced them to be more attentive to their *purdah* in some ways. They had to redefine their strategies around the *purdah* as they prepared themselves to face the next accusation from their communities: "These women roam all over the world untamed. Night after night, they just hang out in the office." A little bit of *purdah* saved these women from the gossip of the neighbours and relatives, and also encouraged their *sasuralwalas* to proudly show off—"Look, our daughter-in-law not only earns an income, she also respects the honour of our family!"

For Chaandni, a Muslim working in an organization with a heavy Hindu presence, this matter was slightly different and more complicated. She knew that as soon as they got an opportunity, her people would accuse her of betraying the community: "Oh, such and such's wife is so wild! All she had to do was start working with the Hindus, and she didn't waste a minute before getting rid of her *naqab*." For this reason, although Chaandni stopped covering her face, she was always careful to keep the *naqab* on her head when she was in the village. As soon as she crossed the border of her village, Chaandni's *naqab*—like the *ghoonghats* and *palloos* of the rest—slid down and made its way into her bag. But people in Chaandni's village fully respected her and her work. They frequently remarked: "So what if she works with the Hindus? Look how honest and loyal she is to her religion."

When the seven of us reached the office for the first time after suffering all the opposition and backbiting in our homes and neighbourhoods, all of us were nervous wrecks. Countless thoughts passed through our heads—Who knows what kind of people we will be working with? What will they ask? We are not even particularly qualified or skilled; will we even be able to speak when someone more educated than us tries to talk to us? In other words, not a single one of us was confident about our own abilities. We were trapped in the inferiority complexes that had been stuffed in our minds since we were kids. We had learned that we were women, we were poor, we were less educated, and that made us weaker and more inferior than the rest of the world.

Radha and Madhulika write: "Somewhere in our hearts, these self-doubts and uncertainties stayed intact until the moment we received our first salaries."

It is not that all these uncertainties were simply rooted in a lack of self-confidence. Some fears were connected with the deep mistrust inspired by the hollowness of government policies and rural development programmes. For instance, after he gave his consent to Radha's employment, somehow, her husband's courage began to slip. He said: "This is an organization funded by foreigners. They will first win people's trust here and then go and sell poor women overseas in the sex trade."

From the day Radha stepped outside, her home became a war zone. Whenever she had to go into another village, she became apprehensive: "How will I do justice to my work here?"

It was simply her faith in Radha that led Chaandni to travel all the way from her village to the district office. She had heard many stories about the attitude of the government towards poor Muslim women. When she had to spend her first night in the office, Chaandni and her husband were afraid that those who had given her the job would force her to get sterilized. This fear caused Chaandni to take a neighbour with her. She writes: "I was repeatedly haunted by the fear, 'What will happen now?' I could not sleep the whole night. The fear of losing my honour was all I could think of."

As we began to shed these deep seated fears, another journey began for us—the journey of identifying the notes of our muffled voices, the journey of turning our dreams into reality, the journey to give and take power with our newly-found vision and strength.

Garima, who started her career on daily wages in NSY, vividly remembers her early days. Someone who was given the title of "dumb like a cow" in her natal home, Garima cannot forget how difficult it was for her to break her silence. She writes: "Making my way through many barriers, I came to Sitapur to start my job. My mother and daughter came along. One of my uncles lives about a kilometre and a half away from the office in Roti Godam. We went to stay with him. I could not afford the fares of the cycle rickshaw, so early in the morning, I would walk from his house to the office. At the end of the day, too, I returned on foot. I did not know the language of the city-folks [*khadi boli*], so I even hesitated to speak in my own tongue. But as I walked on my way to and back from work, I tried to speak with myself in the city tongue so that I could get into the habit of speaking it."

If Sandhya was intoxicated with something in the early days of work, it was with the desire to prove herself. Because Sandhya was not selected for the position of a field-level worker, she tried hard to get just about any work in NSY. After her continuous efforts, she got a chance to oversee a literacy centre. Sandhya got tremendous satisfaction from this work, but the salary was so little that she was ashamed of even telling her family about it. She was also afraid that she might be removed from her position after the one-month trial period was over. How would she show her face to her family then? In the end, Sandhya focused all her energies on the literacy centre. She decided that no matter what happened, she would show everyone that she could do good and solid work on the ground.

Once we began our work, it did not take very long for us to figure out that what we had started could not be simply labeled as a "9 to 5 job" that fetched us a monthly salary. It was not a mere job; it was a commitment to drown ourselves in a struggle. At first, Pallavi assumed that her job as a field-worker would be similar to the work that others did in Aanganwadis or in informal literacy programmes. But she soon dropped this illusion. She realized that this was a job that demanded labour and commitment. Madhulika's attitude too changed quickly. She writes: "When I first joined this programme, I thought it would be just like everyone else's job. We will work one day, and stay home for the next four. I did not have the slightest inkling that this was not just a job I had begun, it was actually 'community work.'"

The Chains of Casteism: So Cruel, So Poisonous!

> I used to think that [NSY] was just for Harijans, but there are people of all castes here and most are Pandits...Wherever you see from the office to the field, you will rarely find a Harijan...In our meetings, there were many discussions about caste difference...But afterwards, when we were "released" from work, people would get angry—"If I come from a high caste, how is that my fault? They should send all these lower caste people to eat in the homes of castes who are even lower than them. Then we will find out the truth." All this talk filled me with pain. I used to think.., 'If I hadn't chosen to work here, no one could make me listen to this bitterness.'
>
> — From Madhulika's diary

When Sandhya was not chosen for the position of a fieldworker in the selection process in 1996, her self-respect took a big blow. After all, she had already operated an informal literacy centre before her marriage, so she was confident that she had more work-related experience than others in the pool. Secondly, since childhood Sandhya had considered herself superior than others because she was a Brahmin. Not to be selected as a fieldworker was so humiliating for Sandhya that she seethed with anger. She writes, "From the beginning, I was doubtful whether I would be selected for the position. I had heard that this organization just works for the Dalit castes, so they are the ones who will work in it, too. In the end, that is also the reply I got. Everyone said, 'Workers from upper castes will not be selected.' Hearing this made me very sad. I was also angry that they selected Madhulika, who had just passed eighth grade, but they refused to give me a position even though I had operated a literacy centre before. I felt that they were siding with the Chamar, because everyone associated with the programme was also Chamar."

If we reflect on our collective journey to date with a bitter honesty it would not be inaccurate to say that Sandhya's initial tears of anger were symbolic of those pointed stones and deep wounds that all of us have experienced in different forms by living in the swamp of casteism, and from which we have not been able to fully emerge even today.

Many values and beliefs shackled our feet, but none were heavier than the chains of caste and religion. Since childhood, we had eaten with great relish the *prasad* of casteism from the plate of religion and purity. How could we simply throw that plate away just because someone told us to? It is quite obvious that since the most delicious *prasad* often lands up on the plates of the Sawarns, they are also the ones who find it most painful to get rid of their plates. After all, if we are forced to share the best dish sitting in our bag with someone we have always considered lower than ourselves, it is not hard to feel the pain. But if a dessert cooked in the syrup of high and low is thrown at someone out of pity, accepting that food also smashes self-respect, doesn't it?

In our meetings, someone would frequently raise the question, "Why does our organization work only among the Dalits and Other Backward Castes? Has no one else, besides them, been oppressed or exploited?" Sandhya repeatedly pointed out that injustices are being wreaked on poor women of all castes, so why is the organization turning a blind eye toward upper caste women? By contrast, others among us found the organization's claim that it works with Dalit and exploited groups to be hollow and papery. Madhulika often felt that the organization was filled with nothing but Sawarns all the way from the district office to the villages. "Wouldn't it have been wonderful," she thought, "if there had been literate women among our Dalit castes as well. If our Dalit communities had only bothered to educate their daughters, they would be working in this organization today instead of so many Sawarn Hindu women." Similarly, when Chaandni felt suffocated by the domination of caste Hindus in the organization, she blamed her own community for keeping their girls in seclusion and out of schools. She thought to herself that if only they had been allowed a chance to get some education, Muslim women and girls would have done so well in NSY.

Now we realize how easily we explained away the acute under-representation of women from marginalized castes and classes in NSY by blaming those very groups—for being backward, for chaining their women and girls to their homes, and for depriving their women of education and of opportunities to earn a living. But if all this had been so easy to accomplish, we would have dragged all of them out of their homes and handed them jobs in women's NGOs between 1996 and now! The truth is that girls from these communities cannot study even when their parents want them to. Why is it so? Why is it that, despite all the drum-beating about reservation policies, Dalit women cannot find jobs anywhere? Why is it that, even in those NGOs that flourish in the name of Dalits and in the midst of Dalit communities, the organizational spaces are full of paid officials from upper castes all the way from the office to the fields? It was only gradually that we started understanding the complex and tight knots associated with these perennial questions.

Sandhya tells a story about a Brahmin teacher she had in school. He always made a point to taunt his Dalit students—"What can the government do just by reserving a space for you? Let it grant you as many spaces as it wishes. You can't move an inch unless I teach you!"

Radha, who came from the only "untouchable" family in her village, remembers similar humiliations that wounded her heart as a child, and the memories of which still make her shiver. An upper caste school master often beat her before the whole class, and as he did so, he insisted on announcing to the class, "These Chamar and Paasi have no brains." Radha felt that the school master did not want to teach her because she was from a lower caste; it was only the Kurmi children he wanted to teach and explain things to. If there was an opportunity, for example, to recite a poem or to be the monitor of the class, the schoolmaster gave the first chance to the Kurmi children. Radha hated all this. It made her very angry. But she could never gather the courage to say anything to Masterji.

Wrapped in the stench of casteism and classism, such humiliations and indifferences have greeted us at every step since we were children. While Sandhya automatically received respect from her society for being born a Brahmin, Radha was constantly subjected to new injuries and extremely painful slurs for being born a Paasi. We often notice how women's organizations find funding in the cities and march into our villages in the hopes of finding bold, fearless Dalit women who can mobilize, enlighten, and lead the rest of their communities out of their misery. Rarely do they recognize the different histories that make it impossible for all of us to feel fearless in the same ways. For those of us who have been communally beaten down and humiliated in these villages, the work of transforming these social spaces is extremely challenging. Even though we come from the same places and do the same work, the complexities of our caste, class and religious locations make our experiences and struggles as activists radically different from one another's. Whereas Sandhya can always take for granted the respect that is accorded to her just for being a Brahmin daughter-in-law, Radha is always prepared for someone to scorn her: "Oh, is she the wife of that same Paasi who gambles all the time?"

Similarly, Garima gets praised by her community when she starts a campaign against state sponsored liquor because people see her as the daughter of an alcoholic Brahmin who stole Garima's childhood from her. But how ironic that Madhulika is forced to withdraw from the same campaign because upper caste Hindu men can't stop asking her contemptuously, "Who are you to prevent us from drinking and gambling when you can't stop your own husband from doing so?"

The Venomous Rituals of Food and Drink

Every time we wrestled with our inner dilemmas, we were forced to face the extent to which our own minds were locked within the prison walls of caste and religion. When we first joined NSY we were sceptical. We wondered why there were always pretensions of eating and drinking with people of all castes and religions. We sarcastically asked, "How and when did working among other castes and communities come to mean that we should eat and drink with them in our or their homes?" Whereas Sandhya, Garima, Pallavi and Shikha, who had come from Sawarn backgrounds, were disturbed by the fact that they had to eat and drink with members of all castes in NSY, Radha's and Madhulika's hearts were eaten alive by the worry that someone would hurl an insult at them for being Dalit. Some segregation from Raidas and Paasi was also practiced in Chaandni's Sunni Muslim community, but it was not as extreme as in the Sawarn Hindu families. But all the workers, including Chaandni, were speechless with horror when we saw a Bhangi cleaner working in the office-kitchen one day. None of us could tolerate the sight or the idea of a Bhangi worker cooking for us in the kitchen. So desperately did we want to keep our jobs and earnings, however, that we all remained quiet. Not a single one of us had the guts to openly express a negative response.

This was just the beginning. It did not take very long for us to understand that the journey we had embarked upon to end oppressions through our work was closely related to the kingdom of eating and drinking rituals. To recount another incident from our early days: Madhulika had gone for a meeting to Ratosia village. After the meeting, a woman from the Maurya caste insisted on inviting her to her house. The Maurya woman had thought that Madhulika was a resident of the Brahmin dominated village of Rampur. Thus, she served tea to Madhulika very lovingly. Madhulika had learned from her childhood to always wash a vessel in the house of a Sawarn after using it. So after finishing her tea, Madhulika began to wash her cup. The Maurya woman immediately snapped: "Oh, so you are one of those Chamars. Never make this kind of mistake again. Always tell people what your caste is."

After hearing these words, Madhulika, who had been reluctant to accept the invitation in the first place, became even more hesitant to eat and drink among other castes. On an intellectual level, she understood very well by whom and for whose gains the structure of high and low castes had been created. Yet, the comment made by the Maurya woman made her feel as if she had committed an unforgivable crime.

If we place some of the experiences of the Sawarn fieldworkers against the disturbing backdrop of Madhulika's experience, another dimension of the picture emerges. When Sandhya cut back on her segregation from Dalit castes with respect to food and drink, then Shakuntala of Kamalpur village remarked with a deep satisfaction, "When you eat or drink anything in one of our homes, it makes us infinitely happy!"

It is hard to say whether Shakuntala said these words simply because there is a relationship of mutual respect and affection between her and Sandhya, or whether her words betray a bitter desire to express gratitude to the "high-born" Sandhya for accepting her as a friend. Perhaps there is a little of each, but the end result is the same: While Sandhya receives praise, affection, respect and positive energy for breaking the repulsive rules of eating and drinking, Madhulika pays the price for breaking the same rules by being humiliated by a higher caste woman. The hatred that she saw for her caste in the eyes of that Maurya woman wounded Madhulika so much that she vowed to never even drink a drop of water in any house she went to for her work. She did not want to give anyone a chance to ask what her caste was. After being forced to swallow the Maurya woman's insult, Madhulika stopped nurturing any more illusions. Whenever she saw Sawarn workers in her office, she couldn't help thinking: Who knows how much they have really been able to rid themselves of caste intolerance? Maybe they are keeping it aside just for the period they are working in the office."

Radha expresses similar sentiments in her diary: "I did not experience so much intolerance with respect to eating and drinking in NSY, but sometimes our personal conversations broke my heart. It appears as if people are obligated to not show their intolerance in the office. But once the boundary of that space is crossed, it is easy to see for ourselves how much anyone has been able to change herself. It is worth asking if anything has actually changed, or does everything always pretty much stay where it always was?"

An honest assessment will tell us that these questions are not that distant from reality. Garima acknowledges by giving her own example that she does not mind drinking tea or water in the homes of people who are lower than herself in the caste hierarchy, but she does not know why she cannot bring herself to eat anything in the same homes. For example, on the festival of Gudiya one year, Madhulika very lovingly cooked some *ghughri* and brought it over for everyone. But Garima could not even bear the thought of putting it in her mouth. It is challenging to accept our own inner weaknesses before the group, and we respect Garima for sharing this truth so honestly with all of us. Even so, when Garima was narrating this story, Radha and Madhulika were watching her face intently, as if trying to say: "How could you not make your heart change even after working with us for so many years? How could you not eat the *ghughri* that Madhulika had made with so much love and labour for all of us?" But neither of them actually said anything. In part, this was because not saying anything has become an old habit now, and partly because it is extremely difficult for all of us to challenge each other on the question of caste difference even to this day.

When these struggles crossed the boundaries of the office and began to reach our homes and villages, the pains and challenges associated with them started creating even more complications. Radha writes: "I had almost forgotten about the petty differences of caste and creed. But then an incident occurred that made my insides tremble. Once a village woman called Roopa went to Garima's house. Garima's husband just asked her to leave. Even though she was a field activist, Garima just let her husband mistreat the Dalit woman. She didn't answer him back even once. Why?"

It would be wrong to suggest that Sawarn workers made no efforts to change such situations in their homes and families. There were many confrontations and quarrels. One day, when Pallavi brought a co-worker from the Raidas caste to her home, her father-in-law asked the visitor, "Bitiya, what caste are you from?" Before she could reply, Pallavi snapped in a sharp tone—"She is a Raidas." At that moment, Pallavi's temper silenced her father-in-law, but he created a big scene later.

Even as they oppose casteism in their own homes, Pallavi, Sandhya and Garima often find themselves bogged down in the vicious swamp of casteism. Sandhya asks whether change will come simply by eating in the homes of all castes? Why don't lower caste individuals eat in the homes of those whom they treat as lower than themselves? What kind of a structure is it? Where and how did it all start? Why does it persist despite all the laws that have been created to undo caste discrimination?

As hard as it is for Sandhya to see them, there are other aspects connected with these structures as well—for example, the profound ways in which the chains of caste discrimination shackle our personalities. The pain of untouchability that greeted Radha from her early childhood stands in direct opposition to the social honour and privileges that Sandhya happily embraced as perks of her upper caste membership. How can we ever overlook the influence that these contrasting realities have had on these two women's personalities and confidence? As we think about these issues, we find our past to be hopelessly entangled with our present and future.

Communal Untouchability: Yet Another Gulf

When it comes to Islam, there remains an utter confusion in our Hindu dominated women's organizations. In the process of writing this book, the only Muslim in our collective, Chaandni, played a critical role in enabling us to develop a better understanding of the Muslim community. One of the most meaningful things that Chaandni's presence facilitated was an open discussion of the beliefs that had crawled and lived inside our hearts since our childhood, and separated the Hindus from the Muslims. When our conversations happened, we hung our heads with bewilderment and shame. We could not believe the lies that were stuffed into our heads by our own elders and members of our so-called civilized society. Garima remembers, "I resented the vessels and clothing of Muslims even more than I resented those of Chamars."

Even Radha, who had suffered horrible forms of caste discrimination, did not remain untouched by the hatred against Muslims: "What I had learned before was that followers of Islam are very harsh people. They are always united and they do not have any respect for the Hindus...Whenever I saw a woman covered in a black *burqa* from head to toe, I used to tremble at the thought of how these people's behavior must be. My heart was filled with the idea that Muslims are very filthy people. We should not even drink water in their homes."

Madhulika writes: In my home, members of Muslim community visited frequently. We socialized with them, but did not eat or drink with them. We were told, "Don't go inside their homes. Don't eat or drink in their places." Amma used to say—"These people are very dirty. They use water when they urinate, but when they go for a bowel movement, they just use *toti wala lota*. They don't even wash their hands."

When Madhulika, who was brought up on these ideas, joined the women's organization, she became friends with a woman called Noor. In the initial five years Noor was the only fieldworker in the programme from a Muslim community. Madhulika spent a lot of time in Noor's house. Noor also visited Madhulika's home in relation to work. Whenever Noor was asked to eat in Madhulika's home, she did, but Madhulika found it very difficult to do the same in Noor's home. Noor was familiar with the attitudes of Hindus with respect to her religion, so she never insisted too much on eating. A couple of times she asked Madhulika to eat, but Madhulika did not feel like doing so.

Similarly, a man named Abid frequently visited Sandhya's house when she was a little girl. She called him Mama. He ate and drank in her home, but his vessels were always kept apart. Once Sandhya went to Abid Mama's home on Eid. It was a holiday. How could Mama send back his niece without feeding her something? With great affection, Mami [Abid's wife] brought some sweets for Sandhya to eat. She insisted, "Today, I won't let you go without eating something."

Sandhya started crying. Her heart was seized by just one fear: "These Muslims are very fierce people. They might kill me with a knife." She was also apprehensive that if she ate in their house on the day of their festival, they would force her to become a Muslim. Sandhya wrote—"I did not want to become a Muslim at any cost, otherwise I would have also been fed like Abid Mama in separate utensils."

So, even on the very day of Eid, Sandhya rejected the food that Abid Mama and Mami offered her so lovingly because that stubborn childhood mind did not want to become a Muslim under any condition. But even as a child, this incident disturbed Sandhya. She was burdened by the question of why she was prohibited from eating what was cooked inside Abid Mama's house, but when he brought over food that was bought in the market, it was accepted in her house. Sandhya raised this question before her Nani once, but did not receive any response.

When so many misunderstandings had been stuffed inside the six Hindu writers from their early childhood, how could the mind and heart of Chaandni who was breathing in the same environment, remain untouched by this politics of hate? In her home, in her neighborhood, in the school—everywhere she learned the same thing—that all Hindus consider Muslims to be untouchable. Conversely, Chaandni was also taught that her Muslim community was higher and better than the Hindu community. This was not all. Along with the gulf between Hindus and Muslims, Chaandni had also deeply internalized caste discrimination. She made it a point to stay away from Bhangis and castes that raised pigs. She feared that she would become untouchable if she were touched by them.

Once, four Muslim women from an organization in Lucknow came to conduct a three-month long *chikan*-embroidery training programme in Sahjanpur village. Sandhya, who was playing an active role in this programme, found herself in a big quandary. All the while the programme was on, she remained anxious about what would happen if the four trainers arrived at her doorstep as guests some day. She was concerned that, at the very least, she would have to invite them in for tea and snacks. But what would happen if one of her family members raised an objection or insulted any of them? Eventually, the day came when the four trainers decided to drop by Sandhya's home. Somehow, Sandhya mustered the courage to offer *chai* and food in her own utensils. Her family members also found it impossible to say anything against these esteemed visitors from the city, and the visit concluded without any untoward incident.

This whole incident forced Sandhya to reflect on religious intolerance and class difference. She wondered whether she could have invited a Muslim woman who was a manual labourer into her house and offered her tea in her own vessels with the same kind of respect that she was able to show towards the trainers? Absolutely not. And it was here that we felt with an unprecedented intensity the degree to which the politics of purity that are associated with caste and religion are also inseparable from class discrimination. If a low caste person is placed in a high position and is wealthy, then the importance of his or her caste and religion diminish and our society gets guided by money and position. Garima laughingly comments: "If Mayawati[1] were to invite them over for dinner right now, all the Thakurs and Pandits would rush to her house."

But such superficial egalitarianism has its limits. For example, if an upper caste district magistrate behaves in a down-to-earth and non-arrogant manner, everyone praises him for being a good and simple man. If his place were to be taken by a Raidas district magistrate, however, the same people would say, "Oh, that Chamar! He is such a dumb idiot."

The Next Phase of the Journey

> When I placed myself in the shoes of upper caste people and thought about a caste that was way below me [Bhangi], then I understood how, when and where others might feel hurt by the things I do. It is amazing how people such as me who are at the bottom are also trapped in this structure... Will we ever be able to rid ourselves from the term "untouchable?" ..Islam [is] quite special in this respect. Muslims do not have anything like untouchability, although there are many castes.
>
> —From Radha's diary

"We are opposed to casteism and communalism in every form." This is not merely a rule or principle in the women's organizations with which we have been associated—it constitutes one of their "non-negotiable" points—that is, it is a condition on which the organizations do not negotiate or compromise with anyone. In our office, in our meetings, in our trainings, and in what we eat and drink and do, one cannot see anything that resembles casteism or communalism. But we must still ask whether merely making this into a condition gives us enough basis to claim that our Dalit workers do not face acute discrimination? Can the formal creation of non-negotiable conditions by itself ensure the elimination of casteism and classism from an organization? Or do we all need to do something that forces us to work carefully and seriously on this issue beyond the limited spheres of our meetings, discussions and trainings? There has been no lack of discussions or exchanges of viewpoints on all matters—whether it is reservation policies or inequitable distribution of resources and facilities. But do we ever pause to evaluate whether any of these have enabled us to make a "real" difference? How far have we managed to come? Exhausted and bored with these endless meetings and discussions on casteism and untouchability, Radha and Madhulika often say, "Those of us who are at the bottom, are at the bottom. Now, let us stop these discussions."

Why is it that our two most dynamic and influential Dalit activists are the first to get drained by our caste-talk? Because they repeatedly feel that although people associated with the programme pretend to not practice caste discrimination, the reality is something else. If hearts had really changed after seven years of work, a puzzled Garima would not be sitting in Madhulika's house with a *kachori* in her hands, thinking—"Gosh, how am I going to eat this?" Similarly Chaandni would not have been forced to say after eating the *kachori* that today was the first day she could bring herself to eat something in a Raidas home. Nor would we see the faces of Sawarn workers tightening every time the issue of caste discrimination was mentioned.

Whenever issues of caste discrimination arise, workers from Sawarn castes respond by saying something in their own defense or clarification. We also hear again and again that Sawarn Hindus are not the only ones to practice untouchability. After all, the Raidas and the Muslims also refuse to eat in the Bhangi homes. The question is this: Will arguments based on the discriminatory practices of "others" in our own defense help us much in advancing our own struggle? Rather than looking for new arguments in self-defense, is it not possible for us to use these conversations for soul searching in the same way that Radha struggles by reflecting on the interrelationships between Bhangis and Paasis? It is quite significant that Radha, who has suffered the wounds of untouchability herself by growing up in the midst of Sawarn Hindus, used her own pain as a vehicle to recognize that Islam does not create untouchables. No one else in our group was able to connect these experiences of casteism and communalism so easily and naturally.

At some time or another, all of us went through similar moments of self-reflection and soul searching in this collective process. Why did so many distances persist among us despite working and spending so much time with each other year after year? Whenever we confronted this reality, we acutely realized how difficult it had been to release ourselves from the values and fears that were instilled inside us in the name of religion and purity. But our struggles with these messy questions have also loosened many knots in our heads and hearts. Once again, the destruction of the Babri mosque and the slaughter of Muslims in Gujarat became the focal points of our conversation, and we saw how attempts are being made to fill our children's brains with the same communal hatred and fears that were stuffed in our brains once.

We also started seeing all over again how struggles in our personal lives are so intimately tied to the kinds of deprivation and injustices that organizations such as Sangtin commit themselves to fight against in the outside world. We learned to accept the reality that despite going through the same process of training in an NGO, it is impossible for field-workers from Dalit and Sawarn backgrounds to emerge as activists in the same ways. For instance, the absences of opportunities and resources that Radha faced in her personal life often make it necessary for her to labour a lot harder than Sandhya to learn everything. At the same time, it is precisely these deprivations and struggles that give Radha a vision, a perceptiveness and a sensitivity that allow her to enter more deeply into the layers of social differences than any other member of our group.

Wrestling with these issues of discrimination has taught us a lot about our work, experiences, needs and limitations. Today we can say with complete confidence that unless women's organizations working on gender discrimination seriously address the differences of caste and religion, unless they connect all these structures with the politics of families, values and class—until then they cannot honestly claim to have conversations with Dalit and disadvantaged women about the issues of equity and equality.

Notes

[1] Mayawati, a Dalit woman politician, was serving as the Chief Minister of Uttar Pradesh at the time this statement was made.

Cracking Cages, New Skies

People of my village often said with pity, "First, she doesn't have a father; second, her mind is too slow. In today's world, [she] cannot survive." But there were reasons behind my silence...When I was little, Amma told me that ..if Pitaji had remained quiet when he was being attacked, it would have saved our fate...From that time on I vowed to remain silent... But when I started working, I found myself in an entirely different environment. Whatever was inside me, I started saying it loudly. I forgot what Amma had taught me.

— From Sandhya's diary

From the beginning, I faced a lot of discrimination—do not go outside, do not laugh, do not eat good food, do not talk back...but work like an animal—whether at home, or in the fields. There were no rules against working too hard...During my early days at work I was fearful. I couldn't look at others straight in the eye. But gradually, I left the fear behind. Now, I am afraid of nothing. No matter who is in front of me, I cannot remain silent.

— From Madhulika's diary

Since I began working, I have traveled in approximately twenty districts. I got opportunities to learn and teach...my understanding of the world grew—I learned about the kinds of social injustices that women are subjected to...about the legal rights that ordinary people have, or don't have...As I learned, I found strength and courage inside me—the courage to speak...the courage to confront people such as police officers... the courage to build dreams to change this world.

— From Pallavi's diary

Since our childhood we had been told that women just gossip aimlessly, that they do not possess anything resembling a brain, and countless other statements of the same sort! But as our work with NSY enhanced our capabilities, our deep-seated fears and inferiority complexes began to vanish. Now no one could tell us that we did not have the ability to accomplish anything. We knew well that we were no less than anyone else; we understood that the only thing one needs to get is the right chance and the right environment. This does not mean that we did not struggle; we fought many battles, both personal and at the level of the society. Through these battles, we came to understand and scrutinize our work and gained the inspiration to give it the new momentum and direction that it constantly required. Our battles also taught us to identify our limits, which always helped us to keep everything in perspective and to remember how much of our journey still remained.

Soon after we began our work at NSY, we undertook the task of transforming the tradition of thrashing the Gudiya.[1] In the same Sitapur district where we were organizing to fight for the dignity and rights of the most marginalized women and girls, the annual festival of Nagpanchmi was marked by massive festivities. In these festivities, boys and men proudly appeared with lashes to publicly whip the rag dolls that their sisters made for the ceremony with great love and labour. This festival, recognized by our religion and society, is one we ourselves celebrated with great fanfare in our homes and neighbourhoods as young girls. All these years we had accepted the public beating of the *gudiya* as a part of our ancient Hindu cultural tradition. But when we took a closer look, this festival reeked strongly of violence. It didn't take us long to decide that if our aim was to eliminate violence against women in this area, the journey would have to begin by attacking this grand celebration.

Now we had to strategize what kind of attack was appropriate with regard to this festival? The problem was clear: Was it possible for us to uproot a tradition that had been an object of so much reverence for generations? Even if this could be done, how successful were we likely to be if we simply dug out the old tradition and left behind a hole in its place? Or, did we have to think of a way in which the discarded tradition could be replaced with the seeds of a new tradition, from whose roots could sprout new values and beliefs?

We felt that the second path symbolized a longer-term vision and a more responsible approach to the problem. We were snatching away from the people an old tradition and belief that we were labeling as inferior and violent; it was our responsibility to give them something else in its place. That is why we came up with the slogan of "*Gudiya peeten nahin jhulayen ji*" (Don't beat the *gudiya*, swing it).

As we immersed ourselves deeper in the struggle around Gudiya, our understanding on issues of sexual violence and abuse became sharper. We also got the courage to dismantle the traditions, beliefs and hollow rituals practiced in our own homes. This journey was full of ideological battles for us—sometimes with respect to our eating habits, sometimes menstruation, and at others, it had to do with the intimacies between women and men. In other words, every two steps that we took made us realize that we had to walk two more miles in the same direction in order to get close to our destination. But this realization never discouraged us. On the contrary, every set of footsteps convinced us that we were successfully moving toward our goal of searching, seeking and creating a beautiful new world.

Taking two steps at a time, we have come a long way in the last seven years. In this chapter we share with you some of the stories that have made this journey memorable for us.

After working tirelessly for four years, there came a time in 2000 when we found it difficult to believe our own eyes. On the day of Gudiya in Naimisharanya, a crowd of approximately five thousand people embraced our resolve as its own. When we were pushed behind by a massive tide of people eager to swing the *gudiya*, our eyes were wet. The tradition that we had worked day and night to transform was now changing with a new meaning before our very eyes; and the work of transformation was being done not by us but by the people of Naimisharanya. We were looking from behind exactly in the same way that a bird watches its fledglings flying far away from her nest. Suddenly, in that moment, we felt that the search for a "job" that had initially brought us to NSY was left far behind. Somewhere along the way, we had united to become a part of a long process of social change—a process in which with every step forward, we found our feet entangled in many burning questions and complications. It was amidst these questions and complications that we had to find the way to forge ahead in our personal, domestic and organizational lives.

The work we did on Gudiya brought much recognition for NSY and the local women at the district and state levels. Even people outside Uttar Pradesh came to know of us. As this work received the attention of the outside world, we felt it was necessary to take a few steps back and analyze it carefully. We also considered another critical question: Given our resources and limitations, what kind of activism were we in a position to advance on a long-term basis? The work of changing traditions or the work of improving women's lives? The biggest advantage of this self-reflection was that rather than getting lost in our post-Gudiya fame and popularity, we became clearer about the kind of issues we wished to pursue in relation to violence against women. Our own personal experiences played a significant role in providing depth to our own understanding of these issues.

For instance, on the day of Nagpanchmi in 1997, when we swung the *gudiya* for the first time, a frightening episode happened in Pallavi's life. Pallavi worked as a field activist in NSY at that time. It was already dark when she got ready to go home after swinging the *gudiya* in her two villages. Since it was a festival day, and she had left home in the early afternoon, Pallavi felt that she must go home, or else her family would find yet another reason to ridicule her work and say that she did not even get any time off on a holiday! Outside the village, she found a tempo on the street. Everything was quiet, with very few vehicles visible on the road. Only the driver and his young helper were in the tempo. On an empty street, the driver reached out and grabbed Pallavi's *aanchal*. This did not scare Pallavi in the slightest—she quickly grabbed the driver's neck and did not ease her grip until they reached her village. Fortunately, a vehicle of the organization she worked with also passed through the same place at the same time, and

Pallavi was saved. But she was constantly haunted by the fear that if her family found out about this incident, they would prevent her from working outside and all the old problems would begin all over again.

Whereas Pallavi hid this episode from her family because they would have accused her of shaming their name and honour, the tempo driver narrated the same story before his friends with great exaggeration and pride. In a flash, the whole community came to know that Pallavi was a victim of sexual abuse. When this news reached us, we were enraged. After all, so many girls and women remain imprisoned in their homes because of the same fears of becoming victims of abuse and shaming their families as a result. At that point, no one could stop us. Together, we located that tempo driver and when we confronted him, one of us could not resist hitting him.

Ideologically, we are against physical violence as a way to address our problems, but this kind of strong emotional response made it clear to the community that we might be able tolerate other things, but our women's organization had no room for sexual harassment of any kind. Despite all our efforts to hide these events, Pallavi's name became a subject of community gossip. Only a year had passed since Pallavi had started working for NSY, and now this event traumatized her and reminded her of all that filth and horror that she had seen so closely as a child.

Pallavi writes in her diary: "I don't know why I couldn't gather the strength to look anyone in the eye...I was worried about what was to come. What would I do if my husband threw me out of his house? Perhaps I was thinking this because I had taken up my job by going against my family's wishes... My fear was that I would be ridiculed, and on top of that, my name would be blackened for the rest of my life. My husband refused to listen to me at any cost. Eventually, Didi (Richa Singh) met and spoke with my family members, which saved me from a war-like situation at home...After Didi's visit, no one in my household mentioned this episode again. This was the second big turn in my life." What happened with Pallavi was not an uncommon occurrence, and she faced the situation bravely.

The truth is that the village-level NGO workers working with other women on issues of sexual abuse and violence often feared that something similar might happen to them. Along with this fear came the worry that if their family members came to know about the smallest incident of this sort they would exaggerate it beyond words and force them to leave their jobs. So, when Chaandni started running a literacy centre in a village far away from her own, she was always scared. She recalls an episode from her initial days: "Once I was going to the Centre, and there were two young men sitting in my way. They started singing a song...I was worried that they could be thugs from a famous gang that operated there. Who knew what they would do if I stopped? So I hurriedly got out of their way. I said nothing to anyone. I thought to myself that if I mentioned this to anyone, I would be the one they would badmouth. I also worried about my religion all the time. I knew that my family would not let me work if they found out about this. So whatever happened—right or wrong—I tolerated it in silence."

Whenever we confronted such issues individually or as a collective, we realized that no matter how many question marks we place before the definitions of social respect and honour, it was difficult to transform these definitions while living with our families and households. Often, we also thought that it is much easier for middle-class women workers from the cities to engage in all the talk about kicking the home and *sasural* and shaking the foundations of patriarchy. For workers like us, it is neither possible nor desirable to work with our faces turned away from these institutions. As we forge ahead, we have to drag these institutions along with us. In the early days, this is precisely what stopped us from marching ahead many times. At times, we stood facing our families, at other times, it was our religion, and at still others, it was the community. The chains of fear that engulfed us, tightened and made us speechless over and over again. Thus, on the one hand, we had leaped across the boundaries of our homes to work, and to find new strength and voice as we met new people. But on the other hand, little fears such as "what will people say?" continuously churned our insides.

Recalling this dilemma, Madhulika writes: "In my heart I just fretted about one thing—that if someone from my family heard of this or that, what would they say?...I was very scared that people would say, 'Look, Gopal lets his wife roam around like a wild woman. She just takes off wherever her heart desires whenever she wants to.'" But day-by-day, we learned to put these small fears aside and released ourselves from their grip as we embraced newer and bigger challenges.

Chaandni had no prior teaching experience. When she started the literacy centre in Sundarpur village, the women who came there were older than Chaandni. Whenever she wanted to tell them about something, Chaandni wondered whether or not they would listen to her. Soon Chaandni came to understand that for women who were harassed and hassled in their own homes, the literacy centre was a place where they could open up by talking and shedding their burdens before one another and also in front of Chaandni. Chaandni derived happiness and peace by listening to these women's stories, and by giving them the advise and courage that they sought. As she continued to win their confidence, the opposition to her work in the village declined. It was not long before she found herself getting involved in issues other than what were seen as strictly "women's issues."

Gambling had emerged as a social problem in the village where Chaandni operated the literacy centre. It was poisoning the everyday lives of women. When Chaandni first tried to take on this issue, a man from the village advised her, "Don't get involved in this problem, or it will become a messy affair." Chaandni listened to him carefully, but did not lose courage. She began informal discussions with men in the village and emphasized how a restraint on gambling by them would help them save their resources for the development of the village and for improving its social environment. Chaandni's calmness and wisdom impressed the villagers, and as their mutual respect and attachment grew, a women's collective began to emerge in Sundarpur.

A difficulty that arose for Chaandni was that whenever she talked with men in Sundarpur, some man from her own village always spotted her, and the whole story—exaggerated beyond proportions—reached her husband in no time. One such episode happened when a woman from Sundarpur was badly beaten by her husband. Chaandni went to talk to the woman's husband, but she was afraid that if her own husband found out about her meetings with "other" men, he would demand that she immediately quit her job. When she returned home that day, she had a fight with her Devar. Her husband, too, accused her of every ugly thing that he could think of.

The insults of Chaandni's Devar knew no limits. He declared, "Get out of our house. Build your own home and live. This Chaandni sits among Chamars and Paasis. She leaves the house saying that she is going to educate them, but that's just her excuse to chat with other men. She is going against her religion. Shame on her! Someday she will use the excuse of teaching and just take off!"

But this kind of petty name-calling could not stop the feet that had already marched so far. In the process of working on rural issues, it was essential to have dialogues with the men who lived there as well. However, we came to accept that the social values that made people look down upon women who talked with "other" men would continue to pose problems for us. Pallavi and Sandhya can never forget an incident that happened after the first fair they organized in Mehnagar. After the fair, they went inside Mehnagar to return the materials they had rented for the tent. It was dark by then. The shopkeeper asked them, "Don't you have men in your homes? Why did you come at this hour to return these?"

According to the shopkeeper, men were responsible for such work. What could women have to do with such things? Whether we worked inside or outside our homes as organizational workers, our boundaries as women were already defined everywhere in relation to what we were supposed to do or not do, where, and among whom. Therefore, when we decided to shake the bars of these very tight cages, we were fully prepared to face opposition.

In village after village, women were getting organized. However, they were not being able to establish an identity outside their own villages. Gambling and alcohol were two issues that affected the women of the entire block. So with gambling and alcoholism as our focus, NSY organized its very first rally in Mishrikh. Village women were frequently used as objects of decoration in the events organized by various political parties, but this was the first opportunity that women had ever had to take out their own rally. It was a huge moment for us! Not so very long ago we had been too shy to even say "*namaste*" to people we met in the villages we entered for the first time, but today here we were; to seize our rights and to give birth to a transformed world, we had jumped into the lanes and streets of Mishrikh to deliver our message with our voices raised.

Garima, who was known as a tongueless girl in her *mayaka*, writes as she remembers the excitement and adventure of the early days of work: "Earlier, I used to bow my head when I talked to someone standing before me...whether that person was a woman or man. Especially when it was a man, I could never raise my head to speak. From my childhood, I had felt pressures. I was taught never to talk back, never to answer back to anyone. But this did not continue. I changed, my attitude and behavior changed. Working [with women], I found a new self-confidence. I came to believe that the work we were doing was good and important work, and other people also respected it as such. This belief gave me the courage to speak openly and clearly. I did not even notice when my fear and hesitation vanished. While walking on the streets, too, I became fearless. Proudly, I began to walk everywhere at all times, speaking loudly against violence and oppression at every step."

Advancing Amidst Compromises

> When I started working, my economic situation improved...With it, I also found within myself a new strength that I will never lose. I discovered an amazing energy that propelled me to reflect further and further about women's conditions and circumstances...This kind of thinking does trigger conflicts between me and my husband, but it is no longer possible for me to feel weak at heart.
>
> — From Radha's diary

Like all the girls who are raised in "respectable" homes, we were also shown the dream of becoming a "good" woman from the very beginning. Etched in our hears and minds was the image of the same traditional woman who is economically dependent on her husband and whose whole life is devoted to fulfilling the expectations and needs of her husband, children and family members. Often it became very difficult for us to accept that women have desires, needs and responsibilities that are independent of their husbands and households and that they must have the full right and opportunities to attain these. Sometimes we found ourselves so wound up in these questions that we could not convince ourselves of our own rights and entitlements, and ended up making many big and small compromises.

One such compromise that we made had to do with the honoraria associated with our work. It is a fact that our jobs triggered opposition in our homes, but it is also true that as we brought back money to our poverty-stricken homes, that opposition declined. Our incomes not only altered our economic conditions, but we also gained respect in our homes. But the big question that emerged for us was—who should be in charge of the money we earned? According to the new thought to which we had been introduced, we understood how necessary it was for women to participate in the control over and the decisions associated with all familial resources. Nevertheless, the question of how and what kind of control we wanted to establish on our earnings in our own homes was one that created many complications and domestic conflicts for us. Shikha writes: "When I first got money after starting my job, I went home and handed it to my husband. He was quite happy and asked me to keep it. After all, it was the household to which these earnings were to be devoted."

There was no doubt that given the economic hardships from which we had all come, the money we made had to be spent on the requirements of our households. But how much space did we have to decide which specific expenses of our homes were to be met with our earnings? Wound up in this question, Garima writes, "When my husband used to earn a salary, he handed it to me to keep. So, I, too, hand over all my money to my husband. Then I don't have to worry about it at all. I believe that there should be no quarrels at home over money. The two of us have built a mutual understanding on this issue."

In contrast, Radha has a different opinion on the matter: "I do the labour and bring the money home. Then all of it goes to my husband. If it remains in my hands, I cannot spend it against his wishes. Even if I am able to spend it according to my wishes at times, it is my husband who still remains in control of the money. I ask myself, If I am the one who earns the money, why does he maintain control over it?"

Pallavi, too, charted a similar course before making a different kind of decision with respect to her income: "When I first received money after joining work, I thought, In whose hands should I place my earning? My husband's, my mother-in-law's, or my father-in-law's? For two days, I struggled with this dilemma. After much reflection, I decided that it is my earning, I will keep it in my hands, and only I will spend it. Whatever things I am asked to buy, I will get them all. Even if all the money is spent on these requests, it will be spent only by my hands."

To tell the truth, the inner churnings of many village-level women workers are reflected in the conundrum that Radha went through. The critical question is not who keeps the money, but how much power we have to spend it according to our wishes. Unlike Pallavi, few amongst us have been able to make the tough decision of keeping our earnings in our own control. So how are we to evaluate these compromises that we have made, and are still making, in relation to our income? We have our work. We have the incomes that we make after a lot of hard and dedicated labour. These are very small incomes, but they still mean everything to us. But despite all this, are we really becoming economically empowered?

The honoraria associated with work also create other kinds of complications for us. Whenever some issue causes disagreements or objections to emerge in our villages, women taunt us, "Yes, of course, why would you mind doing what you are asked to do? After all, you get paid to do this work. And we don't."

Sometimes we ignore these comments, sometimes they hurt or anger us, and sometimes we respond by saying, "If we do not get a penny even after working 24 hours a day, how long can we carry on this mission of changing the society?" But the truth is that this kind of bitterness and suspicion taught us something about yet another aspect of the politics of rural development. Because we are rural women making two *paise* for our labour, people find it easy to make us a target of their sarcasm. But what passes without comment is the fraud of millions of rupees and the huge salaries that get distributed in the name of rural development and women's empowerment. These are things against which even village people do not easily hurl accusations. If this is not classism, what is? Do people ever ridicule high development officials in the same way that they ridicule us? If a big officer utters even a single sugarcoated word, people are impressed and say, "Look, such and such is so nice despite being a high official." But it is far too easy to mistrust rural NGO workers like ourselves, and pass judgements.

Yet, no matter how complicated the issues related to work and money have been, the families and communities among whom we have sweated night and day have definitely learned to value and appreciate our work sooner or later. Pallavi's family fiercely opposed her work in the beginning, but their demeanour changed the day when a conflict pertaining to their familial land made its way to the police station. Pallavi had gone to Sitapur for a meeting that day. Suddenly, her husband arrived in Sitapur to fetch her. He was afraid that if he himself went to the station, the police officers would send him home with two slaps on his face. But they wouldn't think of behaving in this fashion with Pallavi because first, she was a woman. And second, her husband knew quite well that Pallavi would be able to confront the police without fear or hesitation.

There was a time when we had had to battle hard with our own belief that women from respectable homes do not go to the police station. Now, we had reached a stage where our own family members came all the way to Sitapur to deliver us invitations to the police station! When big and small household issues started appearing before us in this way we recognized that no matter how painful it was for our family members to give us control over our earnings, there was a big chunk of the reins of the familial kingdom that they had willingly started sharing with us.

In the middle of these challenges inside and outside our homes, we have continued to work on issues of poor and Dalit women, and our work has gained recognition and standing among the rural communities. Our understanding of our goals and strategies has also sharpened with time and experience. Whenever we have focused our reflections on women and workers in the villages, our own problems have seemed relatively insignificant. At every step, we have tried to determine which social battle we have been in a position to take on at a given point in time, and what we have wanted to gain from it. For example, we stepped out of our homes to take on our jobs as mobilizers and we have picked and fought many new battles on the way. However, we have also considered it necessary to balance social values and expectations in such a way that no one can raise a finger at us. In the course of mobilizing and organizing rural women, we have had to consider responsibly that when we as workers have to bear so many attacks in the name of social honour and respect, then how many barriers must be in the way of women who have to do the same rebellious work right in the middle of their homes and neighbourhoods? Sometimes by standing with them, and sometimes by placing ourselves in the shoes of these women, we have had to think hard about how to begin a long-term war for women's rights, one that can attract mothers and daughters, mothers-in-law and daughters-in-law alike and encourage them to join hands without trepidation.

In this context, we are reminded of the first fair that the women's NGO organized on the occasion of International Women's Day in the village of Karauni. This was a very big event for us, but we were so nervous right before the fair, that sleep completely evaded us. We were scared about what people would say when they saw us acting on the stage. If they pointed fingers or made fun of us, wouldn't that also devalue our work?

In the villages where we worked, we were not simply NGO workers in the eyes of the communities, we were also daughters-in-law and as such, it was inappropriate for us to appear in public without covering our heads with our *palloos* or *dupattas*. Therefore, we decided that we would cover our heads during the rally and the play in the fair, too. When the rally advanced, we went crazy with excitement—we didn't even notice when our *palloos* slid from our heads. And at that moment, no one created a storm when our *palloos* fell.

From that day onwards, we have not tried to make any conscious effort to pull our fallen *palloos* back in their old place. We have chosen a middle path, however. In and around our homes and neighbourhoods, we keep our heads covered, but once we step outside our villages, we let our *palloos* and *dupattas* slip. After the incident at the fair, we have understood well that if a process of change is carried out in a respectful and thoughtful manner, it is much easier for ordinary people to accept and recognize it.

There are some beliefs from whose grip we have found it extremely hard to free ourselves, however. On the issue of menstruation, some of us have found ourselves in just such a mental swamp. Since childhood, our heads have been filled with the idea that we become untouchable on the days when we menstruate.

Garima writes: "When we learned the facts about menstruation, I realized that I had remained trapped in the old beliefs all my life. During my period, I used to cook but did not touch the pickles. I did not consider it inappropriate to participate in other household activities. But I still cannot muster the heart to do *pooja* when I have my period."

At times we all ask ourselves: why is it that we have been able to break the chains of all other superstitions about menstruation, but cannot rid ourselves of the beliefs that have crawled and made homes inside our heads with respect to religion? We know that menstruation is not dirty. That there is nothing wrong in performing *pooja* when we are menstruating. Yet, some fear of religion tucked away in the corners of our hearts prevents us from breaking the chains of this belief.

Similarly, the complexities associated with intimacies between women and men have also created difficult mazes for us. When we started our jobs we had never imagined that one day we would find the guts to talk to other men besides our husbands. We quickly freed ourselves from this narrow-mindedness. However, we have found it extremely difficult to modify our inherited beliefs and ideologies when it comes to sexual relationships and desires.

Struggling with these issues all the time, Garima writes: "First, we ourselves failed to understand why a married woman should come close to another man. Then we felt that if men could form intimate relationships with other women besides their wives, then married women could also live with other men. In my opinion, the real problem lies with the institution of marriage, which encourages and triggers the bondage of dowry and superstitious traditions. But after freeing oneself from this mental bondage, it is still appropriate for a specific man to maintain a relationship with a specific woman. Everyone should be free to choose their own partners, and if they don't like their partners, they should also have the right and the space to choose another partner. But I cannot imagine a woman in two or three relationships. After all, how independent can she be in a situation like this? She will merely become a football to be played around with. Before whom will she open the innermost layers of her heart? Who will understand her? These are not simply questions, they are very tight knots that are not easily undone...I still haven't found a way to come out of this maze."

During the course of our work, we have found it necessary to struggle with these issues collectively. For instance, we recalled an incident involving a women called Santosh. When Pallavi and Sandhya found out that she was pregnant with a child who was not from her husband, both became very upset with her. They told her that they couldn't help her in any way. Somewhere deep down, their attitude was rooted in the belief that Santosh was not a woman of good character. In contrast, when an unmarried woman became pregnant, and the news reached Pallavi and Sandhya that her family members were adamant about killing her, Pallavi plunged her heart and soul into saving the woman's life. For the first time in our field—even if it was in a remote village—we were able to loudly ask why this was considered the young woman's fault? Why wasn't the man who impregnated her also blamed for the irresponsible act? And even if we were to follow the social norms and label the foetus as a "mistake," then too, who and what gave us the right to punish that young woman?

Having a womb is one of our biggest sources of power as women. But how ironic that in the same world that we create with our wombs, women such as Santosh are forced to undergo trials by fire (*agni pareeksha*) because of their wombs. By giving us an opportunity to identify and understand the meanings of our womb, Santosh's struggle reinvigorated and energized our thinking. It triggered conversations among us on the subject of women's sexual desires and needs. Before branding a woman as right or wrong, we checked ourselves and asked what might have happened, and found out the circumstances that bound her. Why is it that all the restrictions, rules and regulations have been dumped into the laps of women? Why is it that we are expected to be the sole custodians of sexual purity and all the trials by fire are forced on us? Why, since our childhood have our heads been stuffed with glorified accounts of Sita's *agni pareeksha*? Why was it that the same Sandhya who was completely turned-off by marriage got easily convinced after reading a religious book which argued that women could not go to heaven unless they got married before their death? Why, despite the pleasure and satisfaction that they derived from our salaries, was the first objection that our husbands raised about our work couched in the form of the question: "Why does your job require you to stay in the office overnight?"

Countless questions such as these emerged and forced us to reflect deeply on these issues over and over again.

Hearts Dancing on Wheels

Working for the rights and entitlements of Dalit and exploited women like ourselves has never seemed like mere work to us. For us, this struggle has become the tool to regain all those rights that our society had snatched away from us in our early childhood. For instance, the termination of our formal education was a very painful experience for several of us. We had never even dreamed that we would be able to restart our education after we had become mothers. To do so was a very difficult ordeal for us. All of us had school-going children; after paying all their educational expenses, trying to find the resources for our own studies was no joke. But the strength we derived from our work in the communities gave us not only an insuppressible desire and courage but also a sense of direction for weaving and fulfilling our new dreams. When Chaandni decided to appear for her high school examination, she could not arrange money for the fees. Chaandni's mother had given her a pair of gold earrings—the only expensive jewellery she ever owned. Chaandni dearly loved these earrings, but when it was time to fill out the form for her high-school exam, she unhesitatingly handed them to her husband to mortgage!

In addition to receiving formal education, another dream had been denied to us as women. This dream had to do with riding bicycles and chasing new skies. By the time we reached adolescence, the same childhood that had bound our feet and taught us the definition of a good girl, took away our courage to realize this dream. We had almost completely forgotten it after once so greedily pursuing it as little girls. So, when after one year of working in the villages, the idea of riding bikes to the villages came up, it created a huge dilemma for Sandhya: "In these villages, no one's daughter-in-law or wife even went out for a job. How could I ride a bike? Even the girls didn't come near a bicycle—and I was a daughter-in-law! I decided that I wouldn't ride a bike even if I had to give up my job. But there came a day, when I had no choice but to ride a bicycle to my field."

Madhulika was the first worker among us to buy a bicycle. At that time, it did not trigger any particular opposition in her home, but even now when she gets angry, her mother-in-law uses the bicycle as a basis for her accusations: "She roams around in the whole world like a prostitute..."

In the beginning, Radha was worried that similar accusations would be thrown at her. She was in a dilemma about how to tell her husband about the bicycle. One day she lied that she was going to Sitapur for a meeting, but when she returned home with a bicycle her husband jokingly mocked her, "Oh. Now you will make me raise my head with pride." But once Radha started biking, he did not object again. Radha felt as if a wish that she had held on to since her childhood had come true.

Sandhya definitely had to battle with herself on the question of how she would ride the bicycle as a daughter-in-law, but no one from her family ever prevented her from riding. Others among us had to face considerable opposition from our families. As soon as Pallavi's husband heard about the bicycle, their house was hit by a storm. He said, "Ah, yes. This was the only thing that remained to be accomplished! Go ahead and do it. Roaming in village after village, you have already massacred all the social respect I had. The only thing that's left for you now is to mount a bike!"

When Pallavi bought her bike, no one from her family came to know about it. They just assumed that she had borrowed it from her office. Even so, her husband did not consent to her riding the bike to her field. The day her husband came to the office to take Pallavi to the police station in relation to the land dispute, Richa Singh confronted him. In Pallavi's words: "Didi asked, 'It is shameful for Pallavi to ride a bicycle, but it is not shameful for her to go to the police station?' After a long argument, he agreed not to stop me from riding, but he also threatened to shoot me if he ever saw me crossing the street intersection near our house on my bike." But how could these empty threats stop Pallavi? She simply needed her husband to agree once. Today, mounted on her bicycle, Pallavi passes countless times through the same intersection that her husband once named as grounds for shooting her.

In situations where domestic opposition did not pose a big problem, other hurdles emerged. A fearful Garima could not be convinced that she could even learn to ride a bike, let alone ride to remote villages. After many trials and tribulations, she managed to ride. Once she started riding, an overwhelming sense of adventure gripped her. So much so, that even in her sleep, Garima dreamed of going everywhere on her bike.

Shikha, too, nervously started learning to cycle, but when she fell from the bike twice in a row and injured her hand, she gave up. To analyze our stories with honesty, we would have to ask whether it was just her fall from the bicycle that stopped Shikha from riding? Or was her hurdle the pretense of middle-class social respectability that encaged her from all sides?

Chaandni is the only member of this group whose work at a literacy centre did not give her a chance to ride a bike. Because Chaandni's work was concentrated in a single village, NSY did not create an opportunity for her to ride a bike, as it did for the others who worked as mobilizers. Moreover, Chaandni's financial circumstances prevented her from buying a bicycle. Even today, the dream of riding a bike is lurking in Chaandni's heart, eagerly awaiting the right moment.

For those of us who got a chance to fulfill this dream, the question that emerges is simply this: Why in our rural contexts, where it is difficult for people to survive without a bicycle, was our bicycle-riding regarded as such a huge sin? Just because we were women? Today we have the satisfaction that the new beginnings we made after so many struggles have been meaningful. When in the villages of our respective fields a multitude of girls and young women storm out on their bicycles and ride everywhere, we are reminded of the gulf that separates us from this new generation. Where did we have such luck? When we mounted our bikes as daughters-in-law, we had to make every effort to ensure that our *palloos* remained on our heads. We did not do this because our *palloos* carried any huge significance for us. We simply wanted to make sure that behind our *palloos*, we could continue unchecked the process of rightfully accumulating in our bags the pieces of our newly found independence.

Notes

[1] The campaign to redefine the festival of Gudiya was undertaken in Mishrikh under the auspices and with the resources of NSY-Sitapur.

Challenges of NGOization and Dreams of Sangtin

After getting involved with this work, I have opened every tiny box tucked away in my chest. What I wasn't able to ever say before my mother, I have said it all before this group. Now, my prayer to God is simply this:

O God, just do me this little favour: Make this work bigger than my faith.

—From Chaandni's diary

In the early days of starting work, I noticed that Didi also sat with us on the *dari*. I wondered, 'What kind of an officer is she? In every other organization, there is always a separate seat for the officer, but there is no such thing here. In this programme, every worker receives equal respect irrespective of the position she holds'... But one day, I was forced to think differently. I happened to sit in Didi's seat while writing some notes, and someone immediately asked me to get up. I was worried, 'What will happen now? Will Didi scold me?' No such thing happened. But it became clear to me that day that Didi has a special place that workers like myself can never acquire in this structure. In this programme, everyone from the top to the bottom has a different position in the hierarchy. Even when we sit among women in the villages [supposedly, as equals], we begin to look and act according to our positions.

— From Radha's diary

Hasn't it been only six years since we first learned to ride our bikes and stormed the neighbourhoods, streets and villages of Sitapur? Who among us had imagined that we would so confidently rebel and march out of the same households that caged us, where our work had met with so much disrespect and disgust?

When we were preparing ourselves to write this book, we again felt a sense of adventure creeping into our bones. Would this world be able to see us formerly uneducated women as writers? Would it give us the same respect and wisdom that it accords to all its upper caste and elite scholars and thinkers? Would our readers be able to value the courage and trust with which we have poured out our most cherished and intimate moments, our deepest sorrows and wounds of humiliation, and everything sweet and bitter that we have encountered in our lives?

Another issue that concerned us throughout this period of writing has to do with honesty and confidentiality—the same issue with which we grappled before embarking upon our journal writing and decided that we will not hide anything from each other about our personal lives. We knew all too well from working in a women's organization that it is much easier to interrogate the definitions of honour, morality and justice by giving instances from the lives of others than by applying those critiques to our own clans and families. Even so, we unveiled details about our lives in our diaries and discussions because we believed that we would not be able to advance this struggle by hiding things. We suspect that our readers will read with pleasure—and perhaps, respect—the details we furnish here about our intimate lives and relationships, our sexuality, our poverty, and the putrid swamps of casteism and communalism that we live in. But we wonder whether they would be able to read with equal pleasure or respect our analyses and critiques of women's and development NGOs. But on this issue, too, we were inspired by the belief that if we couldn't muster the courage to say everything even after arriving at this juncture in our journey, then it would be difficult to fight the battles to come.

When we started this work, we had one desire—the desire to find a job and stand on our own feet. After a short time we saw that this job was not just a source of income; it became our integrity, our life's pulse. As we became familiar with women's issues and struggles in our fields, and as we deeply connected with them, our vision and horizons continued to expand.

There was a time when our whole lives were imprisoned in our own homes. But now a new vision altered our world. As we stepped outside our homes, we started speaking with confidence. We encouraged the women with whom we worked to find the same strength and force inside themselves. But the shocks came when we began to recognize from up close the inequalities of rank and class that were embedded in our organizational structures; sometimes these inequalities were related to us, sometimes to the ordinary village women, and sometimes to the big and small organizations trapped in the complex web of NGOs. At times, these inequalities make us so confused and bitter that we lose the confidence to tread our future paths independently and on our own terms and conditions. Through Sangtin Yatra, we have made a first attempt to systematically analyze the dilemmas and complexities of hierarchization and NGOization, so that this process can guide our vision and thought for the next phase of our journey. In this chapter, we share some fragments of the battles we have had with these difficult questions in our journey thus far.

Mazes of Rank, Hierarchy and Classism

> An educated city woman who teaches in my literacy centre knocked on my door this morning. She was surprised to see me looking like an ordinary village woman: "Look at you! Who will say that you are an NGO worker? Why don't you maintain the same appearance here that you do at work?" I replied, "How can I forget the immediate realities of my home and surroundings?"
>
> — From Radha's diary

> When I first arrived in one of the villages of my field, I met Sunanda. She said: "Come, I will take you to Ishwarlalji's house. All important people who come to the village, visit him first... He is wealthy. He has a government job—that's why!"
>
> —From Sandhya's diary

> A big campaign against violence towards women was to be inaugurated [in the city]. I was in an inside room when everyone piled into a car and left for the event. Suddenly, someone realized that I

> was missing and returned to get me. .As we sat in an auto-rickshaw to leave, one of the two young social workers, exclaimed, "Oh, I left my lipstick in the office. How will I appear before everyone now!" Luckily, the other one found a lipstick and the problem was solved. I asked myself: Are these women really going there to talk about Dalit oppression?'...I don't mind self-decoration, but can such women truly immerse themselves in work on the ground? No doubt, they will continue to impress the media.... Can village women like us ever look smart like them? Why would the media ever pay attention to us?
>
> — From Pallavi's diary

The world of NGOs is also becoming a confusing vicious circle for organizational workers like us. On the one hand, we find ourselves ever more articulate and refined while participating in discussions about equity and equality. On the other hand, we cannot turn away from the reality that we—and other NGO workers like us—are becoming more and more distant from our rural worlds with respect to our lifestyles and aspirations as we try to become more impressive in the NGO society. We find it easy to say to the village women that we are ordinary women like themselves. But the truth is that a huge gulf has come to separate us from them. Organizational processes and styles force us to emerge among village women in a special way, which also causes people in the villages to make several right and wrong assumptions about us, and about our associations with government or voluntary structures. If we insist on erasing this distance and remaining rooted in our ground, the affectionate advice we receive from our well-wishers in the NGO sector is: If in today's world, an organization such as Sangtin wishes to acquire adequate resources to thrive, it is not as necessary for us to worry about how much force there is in our work as it is to think about the amount of clout we carry with the big names in the regional and national NGO networks.

Our initial introduction to this deep contradiction and double standard existing in the foundation of NGO structures was sobering. In the beginning, we could not fathom how our organization gave us so much space and the resources to boldly talk about equity and equality before rural women and in the village society. But in the very same organizational spaces where our efforts were praised endlessly, our voices were muffled in the presence of higher officials, and all the slogans and talk of equity and equality were pushed aside. When we tried to open our mouths in defiance, we were informed that the issues we wanted to raise were not meant to be discussed before the officers; whereas in the villages, we had always learned, and taught others, to state our opinions openly and impartially. We do not claim that whatever we tried to say was always correct. What disappointed us, however, was the fact that we were discouraged from articulating our opinions about class differences in an environment where there was constant talk about equity and equality.

For example, inequalities associated with salaries and food and travel allowances have been a subject of much debate among us. In theory, the NGO worker at the field level is deemed very important, yet an office worker at the lowest rank in the organization often draws a bigger salary than the field-worker. Some women's organizations refuse to collapse education with formal literacy from the outset and consider ground experience at par with formal education. But this policy proved hard to implement when it came to determining monthly salaries and honoraria in NSY. For example, the teachers who taught adolescent girls and women in the literacy centres received increments in their honoraria on the basis of formal educational qualifications—that is, a teacher who had completed eighth grade received less money than the one who had passed Intermediate, even if the one with the eighth grade qualification had to work much harder and longer than the one with the higher educational status. It was easier for workers to express their pride in words, "We are not educated; we are made." But in practice, where was the equal status for the less educated ones? There are many other examples of this kind.

For instance, Sandhya writes, "We raised a small question that the big officer goes in the air-conditioned train compartment and the junior one in the second class sleeper. All we had to do is utter these words and the officers started feeling very offended. [Seeing this,] a village woman sitting next to me grabbed my hand and said, 'Don't talk like this...' I thought to myself that raising something as small as this upsets these top officials so much! So when we question patriarchy and men's power in the villages of our fields, and those men scream back at us that their women are getting out of control, why do we get upset with them?"

The basic issue here is that when, as workers who play the most critical role of giving strength to village women, we mustered the courage to articulate our concerns to our bosses, they did not wish to listen. Perhaps this was because we are field-level workers, and get some monetary compensation that allows our families to survive. But it is not simply those who sit above us who are at fault. We ourselves frequently checked our tongues so that our livelihoods were not placed in jeopardy.

If we look carefully, we will find a common scenario. When an organization holds a meeting or event on the public platform, people of all ranks sit with ordinary workers and rural people. But inside the rooms of the offices and buildings, special seats are reserved for all the higher officials. These are the seats which people of lower ranks either hesitate to occupy, or never occupy. These reserved seats are symbolic of a structure in which everyone—from the director, the accountant, and the messenger to the women from the remotest villages—has a pre-determined place. We believe that those who have created these structures have often allocated these places in the absence of and without any consultation with the rural communities. Thus, a lot of energy was devoted to questions such as, what kind of work should be done in the villages, and what work should be allocated to whom. However, there is neither any systematic evaluation of the labour of those who were asked to work directly in the villages, nor were the perceptions of those people for whom we were claiming to work considered critical. As a result, the decision-makers who evaluated and measured our work always remained more important than the people with whom we were directly working to bring about social change—literally, the people who were making this work happen. In other words, NGOs enter our rural communities and talk about the equalities between men, women and other social groups, and they also plan and organize countless trainings and workshops for these communities. However, the very people who excitedly talk about fairness and equality fail to bring themselves to the level of ordinary rural workers, the same people who do the work of turning the goals of these organizations into reality.

In an atmosphere where inequalities of class are spread like nets of thorns in every corner and doorstep, how possible or appropriate is it for us to wage a war by centring it solely on the men in our homes and villages? For instance, Garima notes in her diary: "Women's organizations often take rural women out on various trips and outings. They believe that these women have not stepped out much; getting out will allow them to see the world, to become wiser and more confident. But is it not important for the poorest men in our villages to gain similar confidence and wisdom?"

In other words, can real equality be achieved in our society if we isolate gender difference from all other differences, and base all our strategies and conversations on the gaps between women and men? When we know that the nature and form of gender differences cannot be comprehended in any context without connecting them with caste and class differences, then the inability to raise questions about classism in our own organizations renders our work meaningless just like the tusks of an elephant which are just for display, not to chew!

It is also worth noting that sometimes in the NGO world huge numbers of women join hands on the question of gender, and big groups emerge to address caste politics, but as soon as the question of class arises, the aristocrats of the NGO world dominate in such a way that many things get stuck in our throats before they acquire the status of "issues."

By classism, we do not simply mean to imply the inequalities of salaries and ranks. Class politics are intimately connected with how much respect and space we receive for our work and backgrounds, when and by whom—and when that respect and those spaces are taken away from us. To give an example, we recall an incident that happened soon after the massacre in Gujarat. A well-known organization invited Pallavi and Sandhya as members of Sangtin to evaluate the work being done by some of its village-level groups. When these two reached their office, the officials who had invited them were having a discussion about communalism with visitors from Ahmedabad. Pallavi and Sandhya were stopped and asked to wait outside because there was an important conversation happening inside. How ironic it was that not only were they prohibited from engaging in a critical discussion about communal riots, but Pallavi and Sandhya were not even introduced to the activists from Ahmedabad.

This was an example of a non-local organization. Sandhya recalls an incident that occurred in our own Mishrikh Block. Pallavi had to participate in a foundational training of women that was taking place in Mohsinpur village, but her village was far from the main road and heavy monsoon downpours prevented her from getting there. The punishment for this absence had to be borne by Sandhya. Sandhya writes in her diary: "When the trainer did not see Pallavi, she was furious. She exploded at me and accused me of everything she could think of. The only thing she did not do was call names and hit in the style of our local police officers. I stood like a criminal in front of everyone. Couldn't the village women around me ask her to stop screaming? But no one said anything. They must have thought: 'Why mess with her? What if she loses her temper with us too!'"

Recalling a similar incident, Garima writes: "After working for a while in the office, I had learned a few computer skills. One day, a computer file suddenly disappeared. Everyone in the office started saying, 'Garima must have done it...', I explained a thousand times that I didn't do it, yet they continued to accuse me. Perhaps this is how the powerful bully those who are weaker. No matter how much Didi talks about equality, when the whole structure is created in the form of a ladder, someone has to be higher than someone else. How can there be equality then?"

Sandhya was yelled at for Pallavi's absence and Garima was accused of deleting a computer file because both of them were village-level workers. If a top officer or trainer had failed to reach Mohsinpur that day, or if Sandhya and Garima had themselves occupied higher ranks, would they have been treated this way?

Sometimes all the talk of equality sounds like the hollow beating of distant drums. From up close, one can see that the relationship between a higher official and a field-level worker is the same hierarchical one that exists between an employer and her servant. As the pressures from the funders have increased, so have the threats from our bosses and trainers. Over and over again, we are told that if we cannot show the results that our funders want, our officers will be forced to use a stick to make us work. Many wealthy members of our society make their domestic servants work with the force of the stick and insist on reminding them of their "right" place. In the same way, there has been quite a trend lately to remind us of our right place. These experiences of class-based discrimination often remind us of the lines written by Padhees, a famous Awadhi poet from Sitapur:

Uyi aur aanyi, hum aur aan!

(They are someone else, and we are someone else!)

From the viewpoint of the poorest rural women, the ladder-like structures of our organizations can be seen with even greater clarity. Although the slogan "equal needs of everyone; equal opportunities for everyone" is frequently used, the reality is quite different.

Often, women's organizations send tours of NGO workers from one state of the country to another so that an exchange of experiences among these women can lead to better work. In these contexts, as we have seen, the higher officials of established women's organizations generally travel in air-conditioned compartments, while the village-level field workers or ordinary rural women travel in the second class. Officers worry that traveling in air-conditioned compartments might spoil the habit of rural women. One might ask: Aren't all our habits affected by lifestyles of luxury and material consumption? The biggest irony is that while the national and international treasuries write checks in the names of poor rural women, the bulk of that money does not come close to them or the workers who work with them. Nor is there sufficient transparency in the structures of these organizations for rural women and workers to know how much money arrives in their names in their own organizations, and how and on whom it is spent.

We try to get rural women fired up about how it is their right to obtain every piece of information from the government about its development programmes; that rights to information are important rights for which they must learn to fight. If we are allowed to preach at them for hours about people's right to information and transparency, why do we not have the power to seek and share information in our own organizations about facts such as how much money is coming in and for whom? Unfortunately, the bitter reality is that village-level workers receive very little information about money. However, our least paid and marginalized status hardly prevents the organizations from expecting us to furnish all those services that degree-holding NGO staff from the cities are never expected to provide.

Garima writes, "Once there was a formal request that the field-level workers should be given mopeds to travel to remote villages everyday. The response from the top officer was that "If it takes a long time for workers to get to the villages, why don't they stay overnight in one village, travel next day from there to another village, and then return home?" I was infuriated but who could argue? Had she ever stayed away from her home in her own city? Weren't our children the same as hers? First, we are expected to do trainings and meetings all day and then we are asked to spend the remaining half-nights in other villages...!" The issue here is not why it is critical to stay in the villages. The problem is that these expectations often exist for field-level and district-level workers without regard to the fact that they should also be entitled to spend time with their families.

The food allowance for the participants in programmes at the village level is also significantly lower than the allowance provided at the district and state levels. Garima writes in her diary, "The thinking behind allocating such a small meal budget to the villages must have been simply this: 'What does the monkey know about the taste of ginger? Just boiled lentils are sufficient for these poor people.'" We can claim to be honest with our work only when we can have conversations among ourselves about the extent to which our own economic and personal interests are served by these inequalities.

These days, many organizations do work that produces instantly visible results, for instance, the work of vaccinating or holding public programmes on HIV/AIDS. In such organizations, women are often given a few rupees to participate in the programmes. But giving money immediately raises a host of questions about how this money would affect the mentality of rural women, their attitudes toward grassroots work, and so on.

In contrast to the work of such organizations, our activist work has focused on mobilizing and changing the thinking of women who have been pushed to the margins of our society. This kind of work often remains invisible for a long time, and its results often appear in qualitative forms that cannot be easily measured or compared. We do not pay anything to the rural women for the hard labour they put into this work; they are content simply with the respect they receive from us. The issue that begs consideration, however, is this: In situations where a small portion of the grants that come for these women's empowerment is shared with these women, why do organizational officials have the attitude that "if we tempt the villagers with fifty rupees, they will definitely come." The small amounts of money they might receive are a compensation (however inadequate) for the wages and labour-time on their own farms that these women lose by participating in our programmes. In practice, however, the money is often handed to the women as if the NGOs were doing them a huge favour. Before they receive any symbolic monetary amount for their participation, it is critical that village women see that it is not a favour or a payment for their priceless work; it is a small and symbolic honorarium that ought to be given to them with respect.

The Dreams of Sangtin and Steps Marching Ahead

In the last pages of this book, sewed and woven during the first pause in a long collective journey, we want to give words and voice to dreams that started taking a concrete form for the first time in our conversations. For this, it is necessary for us to momentarily return to some of the same aspects of the politics of name, labour and knowledge production that we began to raise at the outset of this book. We want to start our discussion with three incidents that had a profound influence in shaping our group's thinking on this matter.

About two years ago, a big NGO network organized women's public hearing (*Jan Sunvaai*) on a grand scale. There was a lot of big talk. Many victimized women from various villages were brought before a crowd of two thousand people to narrate, in their own voices, the stories of the rapes, tortures, and abuses that they had experienced. We were impressed. We thought: "These organizers are people with great influence, clout and resources; they will definitely do something concrete and meaningful about the issues that these women are raising. If we narrate our own problems here, maybe our issues will also make it all the way to the hallways of power." We also decided that after these women's issues were sorted out, we would similarly share our views and experiences in public... After about a year, we ran into three women who had participated in the public hearing. Their faces reflected a deep disappointment. They were still waiting in the hope that they would hear of a just sentence on their own cases... There is no doubt that the event of the public hearing was a smashing success, but the women—who were exhibited in that show as victimized "cases," and in whose name so many resources and media people were assembled—merely became tools to publicize and popularize the organizers and their establishment.

We had a similar experience recently in our own district of Sitapur. Some young teachers working in a women's organization were turning the pages of a newly published magazine. They were horrified when they stumbled upon their own names in an article. Upon reading the article, they discovered that various instances of sexual abuse and harassment that they had shared in confidence with the trainer during a workshop for adolescent girls five years ago had been documented in the article along with their real names. Not only had the authors failed to seek permission to use their names, they did not even tell these young women that their private stories were about to become material for publication. Today, these women range from eighteen to twenty-two years of age. If their family members encounter the published material, the consequences can harm not only the women's personal lives, but also the organization that may have to lose these workers forever. The authors and publisher might dismiss the women's anger by saying that they and their families are not in a position to appreciate the significance of such writing, but they should be disabused of such simplistic thinking and asked whether they would have written so vividly about their own daughters if they had shared such experiences in confidence. Would they have adopted the same approach then?

We are not saying that issues of sexual abuse should not be raised in writing and made a topic of public discussion. What we would like to ask is this: If we fail to accord full respect and maintain our ethical responsibility and accountability towards those very people whose lives we claim to work for, will our work have any real force?

The third incident is directly related to us. A comparative study on education funded by the World Bank involved gathering data from three states of the country. The intellectuals who were leading this study are well-known at the national level in the NGO world. Sitapur district was selected as the representative case study for Uttar Pradesh. Four women from our writers' collective became members of the research team for this study. As a part of this, we carried out numerous surveys and interviews in our district, and shared our field experiences and insights in great detail with the researchers. We also got to ride on an airplane, and received a monetary compensation several times higher than our monthly salaries. We are not in a position to assess whether or not we were exploited economically in this process, but there is no doubt that in this whole project, we were the source of raw materials at the intellectual level. We did not have the opportunity to know or evaluate the facts related to our district in comparison to other places; we received no credit for our thoughts and insights; and after the completion of the project, we were not informed about anything that was written or published on the basis of our work. Months later, we spotted an article about this project in an English language newspaper. We saw that there was no mention of the contribution we had made to this work.

If the story had ended here, it might not have been so necessary to make this comment. But it didn't. A few months after the newspaper article was published, we were shocked again: The same researchers were invited to present their research at a special state-level meeting so that district-and village-level workers like ourselves could learn something from their comparative methodology. Thankfully, the organizers and presenters communicated the key points of the presentation to us in ordinary people's language, but we could not understand much about the claims that were made in English in that long lecture. We were even more surprised when our work on the ground was labeled as inferior and immature in comparison to the work being done in other states—on the grounds that kids in the villages we surveyed were dirty, or did not go to school. We were asked to recognize how ashamed our foreign funders would be by our work. We could not believe our ears. Not only did it hurt us to hear our work and integrity being disgraced like this, it also raised a deeply disturbing question for us: Do these "experts" who occasionally use terms like "fools" and "idiots" to refer to the people in our villages really love the "dirty" kids of those villagers who do not make it to school? If they did, perhaps they might have examined more carefully the social and economic processes that are preventing these children from "progressing" before labeling our work as inferior. And they could have at least informed us, before humiliating us publicly, that the work we were being asked to do as research assistants would one day become the basis for measuring and mocking our activist work on a bigger platform. Is it too much to ask that they engage with us about our work in a true give and take?

Although different sets of people and organizations are involved in each of the three incidents described above, for us, they form different strands of the same thread. We realize acutely that in today's aggressive world, where everyone is competing to produce ideas and knowledge, it is not just our work, insights and labour but also our private griefs and sorrows that become tools or toys in the hands of the more prosperous, educated and established people to advance their own names and reputations. The organizers of the public hearing and the writers and editors who published the article on sexual abuse might convince themselves that listening to the stories of these women and adolescent girls has made their audience and readers better informed. But the truth is that these women were reduced to objects for exhibition and entertainment. The organizations and people who received credit by using their private stories benefited from this publicity and visibility. But what of the expectations and trust that led these women to expose the most intimate wounds inflicted on their bodies and souls? Didn't the acts of the organizers, writers and editor mock that trust? How can we begin to appropriately describe such callous disrespect for ordinary people?

On the one hand, as village-level workers we feel that we unknowingly become the medium for these women's exploitation. On the other hand, we also feel exploited ourselves when we see how people above us benefit from our insights, understanding and work without giving us any credit. There is a saying in Awadhi that captures this phenomenon:

Aan ke dhan pe Lachchmi Narayan
(To be called "propertied" after forcibly snatching away others' poperty.)

The upper-tier of the NGO world undoubtedly has higher education than us, they have the knowledge of English, and they perhaps have a broader perspective than us. But when we unhesitatingly share the experiences and ideas we have cultivated and reaped in our "*fields*" by labouring day and night, why is there not evidence of reciprocity, co-participation and co-production from the other side as well?

Whenever our group sat down to imagine the future of Sangtin, the conversation returned again and again to inequalities of organizational ranks and salaries. Repeatedly, the same question resurfaced: Is it possible for an organization to equally distribute rank, money, work, labour and respect to all its members? When we introduce the village women to feminist thinking we say that the labour of a woman who works inside of the house must be valued and assessed in the same way as the labour of a salaried person or an educated and employed member of our society. Similarly, why don't we state that the labour of a block-level activist, who, despite her lower educational qualifications is mobilizing and standing up to help women in the least privileged communities, is at least as valuable and meaningful as the labour of a district-level officer, who gathers funding for the organization and co-ordinates the work being done in various blocks? Why is it not possible to allocate the organizational jobs in such a way that the key responsibilities are evenly distributed among all the members and the question of whose work has greater or lesser significance does not even arise? We feel that in order to wrestle with these questions we have to create a different kind of organizational structure. It is quite impossible to eliminate inequality from a structure that is constructed on the basis of stratification. Let us consider an example: Today Richa Singh is the programme co-ordinator of NSY. Tomorrow, if Garima becomes the co-ordinator, would she refuse to take advantage of the amenities that Richa Singh is enjoying today? Probably not. But if Richa Singh and Garima both had access to equal salaries, facilities and respect from the outset, the questions of taking advantages of amenities and of fewer or greater benefits and perks would never crop up.

Another big question confronting us has to do with the kind of activities Sangtin should embrace or stay away from in the near future. In our discussions, we have often articulated our deep desire to do work that gives us a livelihood while also allowing us to build a social movement. We have tremendous respect and admiration for those who maintain that it is very difficult for the aims and objectives of an NGO and a social movement to merge. In reality, whenever a group becomes dependent on outside grants for its survival, its dependence triggers a series of new inequalities. The issue is the same old one, however: If we don't have the money to gather even the basic resources, how would we build or sustain a movement? After all, no funding agencies give funds to carryout a movement! These days some people work in the villages to earn money and fame, while others work to build and reinforce the grounds for revolutionary change. If we always keep this difference in mind and refuse to compromise our terms, conditions and requirements, can we not create new possibilities within the framework of NGOs?

To create new possibilities it is essential that we do not become dependent on outside funding. We must commit ourselves to the kind of social struggles that allow grassroots workers to have a stable livelihood, without undermining their confidence that they would be able to acquire adequate resources for their work as and when necessary. Today, Sangtin has no financial source on the basis of which we can plan anything for the next three to five years. Struggling to stand on its own feet, our small organization receives a range of advice from friends and well-wishers—some ask us to participate in a big project on AIDS, while others suggest a project on human rights. We are determined to focus on issues that emerge from our own grounds rather than those heaped on us by any funding agency. And it is the people among and with whom we work who will help us determine the standards for measuring our successes and failures. Our experience has taught us that it is impossible to suppress an issue that emerges from the field. And it is only by coalescing around such issues that a movement can advance. If one of our primary goals is to further the issues emerging from our fields, it is also important that we create our organizational structures in accordance with those issue-based realities, rather than by imitating organizations located far away from us. We want to learn from, understand and gain inspiration from the work of stalwart organizations such as Mazdoor Kisaan Shakti Sangathan, Akal Sangharsh Samiti and Uttarakhand Mahila Manch, and use their insights as we chart our future goals and directions.

Our third commitment is towards transparency. When we look at pictures of rural women like ourselves in all the glossy and colorful magazines from around the globe, we wonder whether the governments and media of the world have no other images to display besides those of our poverty, our ramshackle homes, and our naked, emaciated and tearful children. Are these the kinds of images on which our governments and organizations rely to fetch money from overseas in the name of the poor? If our homes and poverty are mocked in this manner to bring in crores of rupees in the name of our own development and empowerment, why are we the ones who remain completely uninformed about how much money is accumulated in our names, and how, when and on whom it is spent? As we make this critique, however, we are acutely aware of the fact that it is very easy to demand transparency and condemn its absence in the abstract, and extremely difficult to implement it in reality. To create transparency within the organizational membership is relatively easy, but how do we share the accounts of millions of rupees with the poorest women in the villages? But then, is this not the same reasoning that makes people sitting above us think that we are incapable of understanding the transactions of the thick bundles of money? They worry that we will be so dazed and blinded by the sight of those bundles that we will lose our old perspective forever!

We want to embrace this challenge in such a way that we can always retain transparency in Sangtin's work. This is possible only when our standards of measurement are always guided by rules and regulations that constantly push us to respect the common people in the rural public, while maintaining complete accountability towards them.

A fourth issue is directly connected to the politics that surround the production of ideas and knowledge. It constitutes a central but invisible element of our work that we also found to be the most challenging and difficult to grasp. We made a small attempt to grapple more fully with this aspect in the middle phase of this collective journey—after sharing and discussing our diaries, and before we began to work on the book.

We took out five days in August 2003 when we tried to place the serious and committed work we had done for the last seven years in a wider context, and to provide a new breadth to our thoughts about international issues. Richa Nagar's involvement allowed us to centre our discussions on several socio-economic questions that we had never had the opportunity to discuss before. For instance, several of us wanted to know how the politics of oil, imperialism and multinational corporations were connected to each other in the invasion of Iraq by the United States of America. From there, many other complex and difficult issues continued to emerge in our conversations. For example, why does the relationship between Israel and Palestine carry so much significance for US politics? What kinds of issues around race and racism have surfaced over time in US politics and why? When we connected these topics with the issues that had surfaced in discussions of our diaries, our dialogues extended in other directions as well. In the global politics of development and capitalism, when did NGOs arrive on the scene? And how did their form change over time? How are struggles on questions of same-sex sexuality in South Africa and other third world countries being articulated in relation to battles defined around class, race, and access to resources? And we asked tens of other questions in a similar vein.

When we linked these discussions with our experiences, we felt that the scope of work done by rural-level NGO workers is defined in a rather constrained way in every respect. We are not given many opportunities that allow us to link what is happening in our villages to the conditions and struggles going on in other states and countries. Similarly, we are not able to fully connect the violence against Dalit women with other forms of violence, and determine our aims and strategies on the basis of that understanding.

Almost every other day, new workshops are organized to ensure that our documentation is refined and polished in accordance with the wishes of our funders. But our long discussions with Richa Nagar helped us to reflect on how we get very few spaces or resources to grapple with a range of socio-political processes that are discussed in academic seminars and make the national and international headlines every day—e.g., globalization and the negotiations of the World Trade Organization, the ever-increasing suicides of peasants in our country, or the privatization of water. As a result, we face severe limits in our ability to relate these processes to the kinds of violence that are wreaked regularly on the bodies and minds of women in our villages. And it is precisely our inability to make these connections that allows established experts and other researchers to carry out study projects "on" us. Sadly, we do not even possess adequate vocabulary to point out the limitations or irresponsible tones that often underlie their analyses.

In Sangtin, we have decided to reflect in depth on how violence that is targeted on women's bodies is interwoven with other forms of violence, and to advance those reflections and understandings collectively with members of our village communities. As part of this effort, we have identified some topics as our starting points. Through discussions, workshops, readings and films that focus on these themes, Sangtin wants to form a concrete understanding that would inform our struggle for the rights of the Dalit and socio-politically marginalized communities.

A multitude of issues begin to emerge as we try to advance these new currents of thought. It is not possible to list all of them here. Even if we collectively tried to give them some kind of coherent order, it would still be hard to decide how to address each of these issues. We believe, however, that it is our responsibility to address some key issues that have presently assumed critical significance for us.

Let us begin, for instance, with the processes of globalization and so-called development that are continuously snatching away resources from the hands of the poorest communities. The resources made available to the rural poor can be likened to a cumin seed in the mouth of a camel; they are too small to have an impact. Even the minimal goods and amenities allocated to people living and dying under these conditions diminish little by little as they make their way down through different levels of the system. Similarly, the interrelationships between the processes and politics of globalization, development and NGOization push us to actively work toward undoing these knot-like puzzles in our own minds. After all, a person breathing in the remotest village is entitled to decide for herself how, why and for whom the whole globe has become a village, and who are the people for whom their whole world is still constituted by their villages, settlements and districts. What kinds of inequalities and social violence does the existence of these two worlds indicate?

Let us also focus for a moment on the ugly face of violence that has shaken up the soul of our country. If the culmination of a debate over the Babri Masjid and Ram Janmbhoomi acquires the face of a nationwide communal riot after the destruction of a 400-year old mosque-shaped structure, and some ten years later, a violent incident in a train compartment transforms itself into a communal slaughter in Gujarat—then developing an awareness and understanding of such tragedy also becomes a critical part of our work and social responsibility. It is only when we place this matter on our agenda that our people would be able to grasp how events such as the Mandir-Masjid debate and the massacre of Muslims in Gujarat shape the communal politics of our own districts and villages. To accomplish this, we will have to develop a historical understanding of communalism. Let us consider the partition of India in 1947 for a moment. At that time, Pakistan was created separately from India, and subsequently Bangladesh was carved out by splitting Pakistan. Without understanding the background and multi-dimensional histories of these events, how can we begin to grasp the complexities of the Indo-Pak partition and of contemporary communal politics? It is high time that the ordinary women and men of our villages be given the opportunities to develop a clear and in-depth understanding of these issues. We believe that we must play an important role in shaping such understandings in our own communities.

While reflecting upon our personal stories we also repeatedly felt a need to sharpen our understanding about the history of the caste system and the various movements that have emerged against casteism in independent India. We also believe that if our main aim behind advancing all of these understandings and reflections is to do concrete and meaningful work in the lives of the poorest rural women, then we must also deepen our acquaintance with the writings and reflections related to women and feminisms, and the various debates and conversations on caste, class, race and religion that have emerged from time to time in various women's movements. Only then will we be in a position to continue our work on the ground without giving up the courage and confidence to intervene continuously in the politics of knowledge production.

And in the End...

When in the lukewarm sun of December 2002, the nibs of nine pens started pouring out our thoughts on paper and transforming themselves into this chronicle, our eyes were wet and our hearts were filled with a pain and restlessness. We had never imagined that a journey that started with remembering and understanding the tears, scoldings and beatings of our Ammas, Babus and Dadis would one day lead us to distinguish between livelihoods and social movements. But today we know very well that it is only when we juxtaposed the stories of our personal lives and saw them with new lenses that we were able to arrive at a point where it is becoming possible for us to honestly re-evaluate the inequalities pervasive in our work-field.

In other words, if we could not build a collective understanding about how Garima's pangs of hunger as a child were different from Radha's, perhaps we would have also failed to see the manner in which the reins of our organization that profess to work with Dalit and oppressed women end up in the hands of the Sawarns. And if we had not grappled with the deep-seated double standards associated with untouchability and *purdah* in our own hearts, where would we have found the insights and determination to question the double standards in the thoughts and actions of celebrated figures in the worlds of NGOs and academia?

The strong bond that moved us from ink to tears has today brought us all the way from tears to dreams. If there are new hopes along with new shapes and colours in these dreams, we are also aware of the new complications, dangers and risks that reside there. And we are also aware that at the very least, this collective journey of creation has united us in a closed fist.

We hope that this fist will continue to become stronger, and that we will gain the support and strength of many many fists like ours. Only then will we be able to create a world where small groups like ours will have the heart to dream big dreams with ordinary people for their happiness—on our own terms, by the force of our own thoughts, and in our own languages.

PART III

POSTSCRIPT

Richa Nagar

NGOs, Global Feminisms and Collaborative Border-crossings

The release of *Sangtin Yatra* provoked a furious, public response from the NSY, Uttar Pradesh, in the form of verbal attacks, letters, transfer orders and threats to take disciplinary action against the authors.[1] This backlash was countered by letters, articles and book reviews in the Hindi media,[2] and a petition sent from Minnesota that created political pressure to stop NSY from issuing further threats to the authors.[3] Below, I present two documents that highlight the arguments and stakes of this controversy.

June 02, 2004. Letter from the State Programme Director of NSY, U.P. to the Chair of Women's Studies, University of Minnesota.[4] *Original document in English.*

Sir,

This is to bring to your notice a research conducted by Dr. Richa Nagar, a faculty member of your department. She did some work in Sitapur district of Uttar Pradesh State in India. She wrote a book based on her work. The book contains personal and work experiences of seven grassroot level workers narrated by themselves. All the writers of the book, except Dr. Richa Nagar herself, are employees of [NSY], an internationally famous programme of integrated empowerment of women belonging to the most marginalised sections of the society. [NSY] is a government programme functional in Sitapur district since 1996. All the workers who are also the writers of the book are community-based workers who were identified by [NSY] coordinators and got associated with the programme since then. The workers have evolved as strong feminists after intensive capacity-building exercises and exposure given to them as a critical process of the programme.

These village workers have also established an NGO of their own by the name of Sangatin. Although Sangatin was established in 1998 yet it did not do much of grassroot work as all the members were full time employed with [NSY]. On publication of the book we are all shocked and disturbed to see that all the experience that these employees had of working with [NSY] has been credited into the account of Sangatin. We are in the process of taking action against this behaviour of our employees. We are writing to you to bring it to your attention that Dr. Richa Nagar has published this piece of work without herself checking the authen[ti]city and genuineness of information. Although she is familiar with the programme of [NSY] and has already worked in the districts of Chitrakoot and Tehri and has documented the work of [NSY]. As per my understanding she knew very well that [NSY] is working in Sitapur and the employees belong to the programme. Yet she neither contacted me nor ever informed me about her association with [NSY] employees on this research work. A number of news clippings appeared in the dailies and the work of [NSY] was reported as the work of Sangatin. In spite of Dr. Richa Nagar's awareness of the reality she did not deny the report and send any note for corrigendum. In fact, it appears, that the two main authors Ms. Richa Singh and Dr. Richa Nagar planned it well in advance to strategically project [NSY's] work as work of Sangatin. Ms. Richa Singh, during our conversation with her, accepted this fact.[5]

I take this as unethical and against the spirit of genuine research. It is also a breach of faith and commitment to social work. Such kind of work and researches are strongly condemned and should not be encouraged.

I would appreciate if you take appropriate action in this regard and inform me about it . . .

Yours sincerely,
State Programme Director

June 11, 2004, Background to Petition: Prepared by the authors with help from supporters in Varanasi, Lucknow, Minneapolis, New Jersey, New York, Pune, Sitapur and Washington DC. Original document in English.

Dear Friends,

We are writing to seek your urgent support on an issue that is flaring up in the Sitapur district of Uttar Pradesh. The issue has to do with [Nari Samata Yojana]-Uttar Pradesh's ([NSY]-UP's) harassment of the nine authors of a book, seven of whom are [NSY]-UP employees against whom the State Project Director of [NSY]-UP is taking punitive action. The main reason behind the punitive action is that these authors have openly reflected on issues of elitism and casteism in women's NGOs in Uttar Pradesh.

The book in Hindi is called *Sangtin Yatra: Saat Zindgiyon Mein Lipta Nari Vimarsh* (A Journey of Sangtins: Feminist Thought Wrapped in Seven Lives) and was published by Sangtin, Sitapur in March, 2004. In this book, seven village level grassroots workers—Anupamlata, Ramsheela, Reshma Ansari, Shashibala, Shashi Vaish, Surbala and Vibha Bajpayee—have released their voices and words to reflect on their lives, on pre-given definitions of honour and respectability, and on casteism, communalism, class and gender politics as it has operated in their own lives as girls, as women and as village-level NGO workers. These seven women have undertaken this writing as members of a small women's organization called Sangtin, in collaboration with Richa Singh (a co-founder of Sangtin) and Richa Nagar, who teaches at the University of Minnesota.

A few words about Sangtin: In every district where [NSY] operates, it encourages the village-level workers to register their own organization under another name so that the work of women's empowerment may continue after the time-bound funded programme of [NSY] withdraws from the district. Thus, NSY-Sitapur is the parent organization from which Sangtin has emerged. The writers' collective published *Sangtin Yatra* under the banner of Sangtin, under whose name they want to continue the work of combining radical activism, rigorous research and creative writing.

A product of two years of labour, *Sangtin Yatra* has emerged from a collectively produced collaborative methodology, where the NGO workers grapple for the first time with processes of NGOization and the politics of knowledge production. One of the major objectives of the book has been to understand through collective writing and reflection, the ways in which empowerment of poorest and Dalit women in the rural areas of Uttar Pradesh is shaped by structures of caste, class and religion; to critically reflect on the seven rural workers' own accomplishments and limitations as actors located in the hierarchical structures of family, village, and NGOs, and the ways in which they want to advance their work on the ground by envisioning their dreams for the future. It is important to note that no NGO in Uttar Pradesh (except Sangtin) was mentioned by name in the main text of the book.

The book was released on March 25, 2004 in a public function in Lucknow by the Hindi novelist, Maitreyi Pushpa, and received significant media attention in the Hindi press in the first half of April.

In mid-April, Richa Nagar left Lucknow and returned to Minnesota. Soon after her departure, the State Project Director of [NSY]-Uttar Pradesh, where seven out of nine authors of this book are still working in the capacity of mobilizers, literacy center instructor and district coordinator, began to launch an attack on the authors of the book. Her main charge was that (a) the book did not give credit to [NSY] for the encouragement and opportunities that it had given to them as [NSY] workers; (b) the authors' reflections on the organizational hierarchy, elitism and casteism in NGO structures undermined the work of women's organizations and (c) the 'truth' of what the women were saying was not verified by [NSY] before the book was published. The authors believe that all these charges are baseless because (a) they do thank [NSY] in their Preface, (b) the objective and spirit underlying the book are entirely opposite to what the SPD of [NSY]-UP accuses it of doing, and (c) the goal of the book is not to present a monolithic truth that requires verification by [NSY]-UP's top leadership, but the analyses, reflection and 'soul-searching' of the authors' own lives and experiences as rural women and NGO workers.

On April 22nd, the State Project Director of [NSY]-UP issued letters to Richa Singh and Richa Nagar in which she condemned the book and called it an example of irresponsible writing which "shows that all the efforts undertaken by women's organizations have been deceitful and dishonest, they have promoted inequality, and are false." The seven authors who are currently employed in the organization were subsequently called for two meetings of over two hours where they were asked to publicly apologize for the contents of the book by issuing letters of apology to all the newspapers that had written about the book. When the authors refused to write such a letter, they were asked to resign. Again, the seven employees of [NSY]-UP refused to resign on the grounds that they had done nothing to violate their loyalty to [NSY]-UP. The organization then transferred Richa Singh from Sitapur to Saharanpur, and verbally defined the transfer as a 'punishment transfer.' Dismissal of the book and *ad homonym* attacks continue, along with verbal and written harassment of the authors in the form of 'charge-sheets,' and outright threats and verbal abuse. A meeting of an 'advisory committee' is being called in where the "issue of Sangtin Yatra" appears as an agenda item. The authors are convinced that this meeting will result in further disciplinary action against them.

We are asking you to sign the attached petition because as the women affiliated with this work put it, "It is not so much a question of whether we get our honoraria from [NSY] every month. We will get by. But if they win this unfair war, no *grameen karyakarta* (village level NGO worker) in UP will be able to accumulate the strength to speak her version of the truth again."

I quote these two documents at length, partly because their different logics and representative strategies make them useful comparative texts by themselves; and partly because they capture the central features of the attacks launched against the authors of *Sangtin Yatra*. The controversy surrounding NSY's response to *Sangtin Yatra* is not only closely entwined with the issues and critiques that the authors raised in the book, it also helps to advance those discussions in crucial ways.

Sangtin Yatra and the Problem of "Truth" and Evidence

The prominent emergence of seven village-level NGO workers in the regional and national Hindi media as political thinkers charting their own future came to be constructed by the director of NSY, U.P., as the uncontrolled behaviour of NSY's employees under a strategic plan devised by Richa Singh and Richa Nagar. The work that the eight activists had done in their own communities, each author was told in a separate letter, was in fact owned by the employer organization which had discovered them and taught them how to do feminism. Accordingly, the experiences of the activists as women and grassroots workers had to be claimed by the organization that was in the business of empowering them. The "authen[ti]city and genuineness of information" that village-level NGO workers were providing as writers of their own past, present and future lives had to be checked with the authorities who had trained them to become feminists. Furthermore, the person guilty of not verifying the seven autobiographers' "truth" was me since out of the nine authors, only my status was deserving enough to be the sole custodian of the "spirit of genuine research." And finally, because both the NGO workers and I had committed a breach of faith by acting against an internationally acclaimed government institution that was officially in charge of the "empowerment of women belonging to the most marginalised sections of the society," it was the duty of our employers and bosses to discipline us.

The backlash was guided by an impulse on the part of the NSY leadership to claim ownership of the experiences and ideas of the grassroots activists: NSY wanted to take pride in their accomplishments and also retain the right to dismiss their critique. In identical letters issued to the seven employees of NSY (i.e., all the authors except Surbala and me), the Director wrote:

> You will agree that it is only because of your work in [NSY] that you were able to step out of the boundaries of your home. [NSY] has tirelessly worked to build your expertise and skills and has given you support and encouragement in every way so that you could reach a level where you can powerfully connect with issues and struggles of rural women and make your voice heard on every platform. Thus, your . . . behavior is an act of betrayal and a gruesome criminal act against the organization. Clarify as to why a disciplinary action should not be taken against you.[6]

A month earlier, Richa Singh and I had already been told (in identical letters and in a more temperate tone) by the Director that:

> We are disappointed that in this book the credit has been attributed to *Sangtin* for all the positive change and programmes that have been carried out by [NSY] in Mishrikh and Pisawan blocks of Sitapur and it has been shown that all the efforts undertaken by women's organizations are fake, dishonest, promoters of inequality and pretentious . . . Highlighting only the negative and suppressing the positive is not a sign of responsible writing. [NSY] expected you to verify the truth of what you were writing and to explore multiple dimensions. And along with it, [we expected you] to highlight the experiences of these women writers with reference to [NSY]'s efforts.[7]

This desire of NSY to establish an ownership over not only the words and work – but also "the truth" – of the rural activists was marked by a deep contradiction. On the one hand, the Director wanted to own the authors' labour as activists and thinkers by saying that the village-level NGO workers could not have written what they wrote in *Sangtin Yatra* if the organization had not raised their consciousness. On the other hand, she wanted the power to certify or discredit their "truths" and to establish her organization's singular and monolithic truth, especially when it came to the authors' critiques of elitism and castéism in the hierarchical structures of women's NGOs.

In order to achieve the latter goal it was necessary to undermine our alliance by splitting the group discursively into the two Richas versus seven rural workers, and by using this argument to try to drive a wedge between both Richas on the one hand, and the remaining authors on the other. The official letters of complaint against *Sangtin Yatra* constructed the seven village-level activists as empowered women who could not have become "empowered" if the organization had not taught them how to stand up and speak for themselves. At the same time, the same women were also constructed as manipulated "subjects" of a "research project" that was forced upon them by Richa Singh and Richa Nagar. Although the director could not resist the temptation to claim Richa Singh in the first category of women who had been liberated and empowered by the organization, she was also compelled to set Richa Singh apart from the village activists. Despite the very different locations that Richa Singh and I occupy in terms of social power and privileges, we were both lumped together as educated, middle-class urban women (read: clever, instrumentalist) whose interests were served by tricking the rural women (read: uncritical, innocent) into co-authoring a book in their name.

The seven autobiographers took immense risks to tell the stories of their childhood, adolescence and marriage; their political coming of age; and their triumphs and challenges as workers in women's NGOs.[8] For them, the central purpose of this journey was twofold: First, they wanted to grapple with the ways in which caste, class, religion and gender intertwine and shape the lives of the poorest rural women in Sitapur. Second, they wanted to reflect on the extent to which programmes that focus on the empowerment of these women have succeeded in addressing some issues but have been limited in other ways, and the ways in which the work of empowering poor women could be made more effective. Each *sangtin* had fully invested herself in this *yatra* – not because we wanted to dismantle the project of empowerment – but because we believed that those who are invested in such projects might benefit from an analysis that highlighted perspectives that are often absent or marginalized on bigger platforms. The journey had made it clear to us that in any struggle there are multiple truths. In this case, the narratives and analysis of the *sangtins* were the truths that we wished to share with our readers. We described these narratives and analyses simply as "soul-searchings," rather than claiming the status of any ultimate, fixed or singular truth for our words.

By misinterpreting and misrepresenting the collective's goals and work, the leadership of NSY not only dishonored the soul-searchings of the autobiographers, she completely overlooked the foundational elements and purpose of our alliance as well as the issues of organizational hierarchies and of unequal access to skills and opportunities that we politicized and prioritized in our work. In so doing, she ended up undermining the stated objectives of her own organization. As Krishna Kumar wrote:

> . . . The charge against the *sangtins* is that [they dared to] write their experiences emerging from this programme without permission and reference. In reality, the issue is not so much of experience, as it is of opportunity and ability. In essence, this book is an evidence of the success of the [NSY] programme, but it also symbolizes a rebellion against the formalities of constituting evidence. The role of rebellion is performed by the words themselves.

> Accepting those words, deriving happiness from their sculpting requires a generosity which if present in a governmental programme can make it revolutionary...[9]

In his assessment of positive trends in education in Uttar Pradesh, Krishna Kumar observed that while *Sangtin Yatra* proves how Uttar Pradesh's "civil society is beginning to register new kinds of voices," the backlash and punitive transfer of Richa Singh demonstrate "how vulnerable U.P. continues to be to its own older personality as a state which resists innovation."[10] While U.P.'s personality as a state may partially explain NSY's response, the backlash against *Sangtin Yatra* still raises a critical question: Why did the coming together of nine women to reflect on the lives, work and future directions of seven activists create such a furore over claiming of names and truths? In a large measure, *Sangtin Yatra* was able to gain resonance in the specific context of Sitapur and U.P. because it made a forceful intervention in the discursive spaces of Hindi and Awadhi. At the same time, the transnational nature of our alliance as well as the socio-political, geographical and institutional locations of the nine *sangtins* made it difficult for powerful state-level actors to either ignore Sangtin Yatra, or to prevent the *yatra* from continuing. In the remaining sections of this Postscript, I explore these dimensions by first summarizing the unverified "truths" of *Sangtin Yatra*, and then placing them in relation to the politics of NGO work, and the ongoing conversations on "globalization from below" and "global feminisms." The final section situates *Sangtin Yatra/Playing with Fire* in the larger context of transnational feminist border-crossings.

The Unverified Truths of *Sangtins*

The *sangtins*' vivid descriptions and criticisms of the internal dynamics of NGO structures definitely ruffled some feathers. But if Sangtin Yatra had done just that, it would not have ignited such a sharp response from an internationally reputed government- sponsored organization such as NSY. What really made this intervention a "criminal act" in the eyes of NSY was the manner in which the collective process led the *sangtins* to articulate the limits of donor-driven empowerment. The process of creating *Sangtin Yatra,* even more than its content, argued for a model of empowerment through dialogue. The travellers come to define our intellectual and political agenda, as well as our own investments in border-crossings – as individuals and as a collective – in an evolving process through which the collaboration finds its form, content and meaning. Solidarity is achieved through active engagement with difference rather than being presumed from outside through the constituting of groups defined homogeneously by need or powerlessness. Similarly, the status-related forms of expertise that Richa Singh and I brought to the collective had to be acknowledged as useful by the other seven activists before that "expertise" had any meaning or value. In other words, the framing rationales of donor-driven NGOs – poor women in need of empowerment through "feminism" as defined and brought to them by more privileged women – was challenged by a model in which the collective worked hard to negotiate everyone's needs, skills and priorities on a level playing field. Because *Sangtin Yatra* launched that critique in a form that refused to isolate the voices of the nine authors or to highlight the "expert" voice of a researcher or higher-level NGO official, and because it was being circulated and disseminated in the political and discursive spaces of the "vernacular" where grassroots NGO actors operated, the critique became dangerous.

So what are the unverified truths of *sangtins* and how do they form a critique of donor-driven empowerment? Even as a "blended we," the collective articulates, negotiates and narrates the complex meanings of heterogeneity, difference and diversity. We show how seven actors – who might conventionally be lumped together as "rural poor women of Sitapur" – self-consciously come together to understand their own lives and struggles as interwoven with local structures of class, caste, religion and gender, as well as with broader processes of development and globalization. In explicitly identifying the ways in which these intersecting structures and processes enable and constrain the autobiographers' agency in their households, communities and NGOs, the *sangtins* try to show how change happens on the ground, bringing vibrancy and meaning to such often abstract terms as "women's agency" and "local knowledge."

For example, we articulate how the autobiographers' varied encounters with poverty, hunger, caste-based and communal untouchability and their struggles to gain access to education were shaped by their different positions with respect to the caste, class, religious and familial configurations that they were inserted in. The stories place question marks on the meanings and idealized definitions of childhood and the "rural girl-child" often assumed by the policy-makers of education and development.[11] The collective also begins to identify multiple forms of violence, the need to conceptualize them in relation to each other, and the dangers of isolating them.

As we narrate and interweave seven stories of motherhood and political coming of age, we analyze each woman's struggle with caste, religion and gender politics in relation to six others. New layers of understanding and consciousness unfold as we re-evaluate the autobiographers' own past interactions in their familial, community and workspaces amidst presumptions and superstitions, cautions and mistakes. We become attentive to the ways in which shifts in the caste, class and religious configurations of each autobiographer's natal and conjugal villages shape not only her own social status and power but also the different ways in which her village and different groups in her village are centred or marginalized with respect to resources and rural development programmes.

Through the examples of men in the autobiographers' own homes (Madhulika and Chaandni's brothers-in-law and Garima's and Radha's husbands, for instance) the *sangtins* recognize how growing insecurities among young men and difficult negotiations over salaries and control over money in homes where male partners and relatives do not have access to stable employment or incomes cannot be separated from the increasing instances of alcoholism, gambling and violence among the poorest rural communities. These reflections bring us back to the structures and priorities of women's NGOs, whose narrow focus on "women's issues" often forecloses spaces for grassroots workers to connect processes of rural underdevelopment and impoverishment with marginalization and disempowerment of poor women. We note the ways in which the inability to make these connections is both manifested in and reinforced by the ways in which many NGOs that aim to empower poor women on the margins of the rural communities end up being staffed and dominated by Hindu and upper-caste grassroots workers, whose critiques of casteism, communalism and untouchability often remain confined to the material and discursive spaces of offices and organizational meetings.

The *sangtins*' insights interweave these realities with the autobiographers' own contestations over seclusion, respectability and honour (*purdah, izzat-aabroo*). Even as we grapple with the linkages among local patriarchies and broader political-economic processes, the collective recognizes the autobiographers' attachment to the streets of their *Babuls* (natal home), as well as the fact that to "liberate" the women in their respective communities, some of them might have to make sure that their own heads remain covered.[12] The activists confronted the patriarchal and violent meanings embedded in the festival of Gudiya and launched a campaign to transform the public spaces where this violence had been legitimated. Their political understandings parallel the insights of scholars who have observed that rituals are dynamic and politically permeable processes that are (re)invented through a succession of contested performances, readings and tellings.[13] But they are not content with contesting the performance simply through their own successful rereading of Gudiya. They recognize the responsibility that comes with the rereading: That when we take something away from a community, we cannot leave a hole behind; we have to provide an alternative ritual, with the transformed meaning, that can take the place of the old one. The eight activists also resist the temptation to slip into a romanticization of their own resistance and return to ask how the transformation of the festival fits into their longer term vision and available resources: "What kind of activism were we in a position to advance on a long-term basis? The work of changing traditions or the work of improving women's lives?"

On the question of NGOization, the analytical process for us begins from articulating in concrete terms the manner in which elitism and hierarchies within the NGO structures parallel and reproduce the very hierarchies that they are ostensibly interested in dismantling: rural-based, less formally educated, Dalit workers find themselves at the margins of institutional spaces in every way, even as these same workers carry out the labour of transforming organizational dreams into reality. We recognize how class differences work to make the "rural woman's voice dependent on the business people of international funding. [Her voice] is heard only when it is translated by licensed middle-people. On rare occasions when it does emerge on its own, it is declared unruly, and therefore, intolerable."[14]

In the process of imagining what forms an alternative organizational space might take, the collective observes how professionalization of organizational structures and processes makes many women's organizations accountable primarily to their funders – who seek certain kinds of reports and statistics – and whose insistence on seeing "evidence of empowerment" often results in standardization and homogenization of grassroots strategies. We also identify the ways in which the idea of empowerment gets visualized as a concrete thing that can be measured, quantified and replicated and where each piece of "empowerment" can be reduced to its component parts. The activists express frustration with how their past work foreclosed opportunities for them to engage with questions of communalism and violence, struggles over land and water, development and displacement, war and imperialism. We recognize how a separation of gender-based violence from other forms of violence pigeon-holes the activists into a narrow political vision; it perpetuates the problems of dependence on, and in turn, accountability to donors (and more immediately, their NGO supervisors and administrators) instead of bringing about broader social changes in the communities of their fields. We also see how the nature of the organizational hierarchies constitutes the activists as "experts" of their local "field-sites," and in so doing, denies them an opportunity to acquire knowledge and expertise regarding processes at geographical scales beyond the villages of their district blocks.

The collective's insights are firmly rooted in the activists' own place-specific realities, yet they deeply resonate with debates over NGOs that are raging throughout the world. The next section places Sangtin Yatra in relation to this wider debate.

NGOs and Globalization from Below: Lessons from Sangtin Yatra

> What role have NGOs been playing in history? They have acted as 'safety valves,' by channeling the popular discontent along constitutional, peaceful and harmless ways . . . they have sought to divide the exploited and oppressed into sections and identities..in the process, obliterating and obfuscating class divisions nationally and internationally . . . They further instill . . . the belief that it is possible to humanize the existing system; and this is done by outwardly taking an anti-state stance . . . Thus while the IFIs [international financial institutions] and international capital strip off the role of the state in regulating the economy . . ., the NGOs agitate for self-help, community development, entrepreneurship, etc., ..absolving [the state] from all social responsibilities towards the people...[With] the massive funds at their disposal,....NGOs have been able to fund ..conferences, four-wheel drive vehicles and even establish institutes for research and policy analysis. Many radicals have found themselves in such institutes as policy formulators and advisors or lobbyists and advocates..In the final analysis, NGOs play the same role that the missionaries and the royal geographical societies played during the prelude to colonization and the period of colonialism.[15]

Chachage's polemic provides one of the most succinct summaries of the many critiques of NGOs that are circulating in much of the so-called third world.[16] The popular perception that NGOs are potential agents for diffusing "development" and enabling empowerment has increasingly been subjected to critical scrutiny. One set of concerns, paralleling Chachage's, has focused on the implications of donor-driven NGOs for survival of alternative visions and local initiatives. For instance, Hulme and Edwards ask whether the interests, values, methods and priorities of NGOs have become so tied with those of Northern-government donors and "developing country-states," that they have now been "socialised" into the development industry. Have NGOs gained so much leverage within a global context because "they now have the social grace not to persist with awkward questions and the organizational capacity to divert the poor and disadvantaged from more radical ideas about how to overcome poverty?"[17]

A second set of concerns has focused on the manner in which NGO structures and project funding, including increased levels of standardization, constrain the spaces for NGOs to learn and grow in response to local concerns, leading to major gaps between advocacy and practice. As the states increasingly outsource their functions to them, NGOs find themselves inserted in a race "to do" rather than to "reflect." As Lewis and Wallace put it, "Finding ways of becoming learning organizations—as well as finding ways to increase accountability at all levels—largely continue to evade NGOs, yet the successful search lies at the heart of NGOs' ability to respond in ways that are truly relevant."[18]

Both sets of concerns can be placed within Kamat's framework of "development hegemony." Kamat conceptualizes NGOization as processes by which development ideology is being reproduced in the resistant spaces of political action—through homogenization, through the politics of funding, through the articulation of universalizing discourses of the modern state (e.g., nationalism, secularism) in state apparatus and in the histories, ideologies and traditions of the intellectual class that is active at the grassroots.[19] She underscores a need to explore how micro practices of grassroots empowerment and resistance can strengthen macro practices of domination, and to present nuanced conceptualizations of NGOs and grassroots social activism that effectively challenge the prevailing tendency to simplistically interpret NGOs either as service contractors, or as manifestations of countervailing power and enhanced democracy.

The same processes that Kamat identifies as development hegemony are also at work in the creation of what might analogously be called gender hegemony. The rhetoric and practice of "gender" have occupied a central place in the complex politics of state and the international civil society that have accompanied the full-scale expansion of globalized capitalism since 1989. International platforms such as the United Nations have come to be dominated by a global "feminist" agenda in which the "subaltern" is "no longer cut off from lines of access to the centre."[20] "Gender mainstreaming" and "poor women's empowerment" have redefined not only the terminologies and terrains of women's politics, but also the sites and meanings of knowledge production. While the funding agencies' popularization of "gender" (instead of "women"), violence against women and HIV/AIDS (instead of infant mortality or price inflation of basic foods), and micro-credit programmes (instead of women's unions or land reforms) has enabled new political agendas to emerge, it has also had the serious consequence of compromising radical politics. Not surprisingly, the interventions made by powerful NGOs have often ended up serving the interests of global capital, despite being largely "feminist in [their] professed interest in gender."[21]

The insights of nine *sangtins* not only echo and ground all the above critiques, they also bring a fresh perspective to these discussions as the activists confront the challenges of NGOization and begin to articulate their vision of empowerment and feminist politics. The collective's analysis confirms that the compromising of radical political agendas and the domination of local priorities by the agendas of funding agencies have been among the heaviest costs that many local activists have had to pay for the NGOization of grassroots politics. It also reflects the activists' growing impatience with an imposed "feminist" agenda that seeks to empower the poorest and most oppressed women while refusing to engage with the increasing marginalization of men in the same communities and neighbourhoods. We resist articulations of feminism that focus singularly on violence against women in their homes or on cultural practices such as *purdah* without simultaneously translating those feminist politics to the communities. In other words, we believe that a feminist vision that the activists cannot operationalize in their own communities is not a usable feminism for the collective.

In articulating these critiques, this *yatra* of *sangtins* connects with struggles of many small groups and communities who are invested in envisioning new forms of solidarities and political agendas—solidarities and agendas that are rooted in their own place-specific priorities and needs while being informed by and engaging with political processes at all geographical scales. This is what makes this journey a meaningful example of a transnational feminist vision, one that might have something to offer to the ongoing conversations on globalization from below.

With the rise of platforms such as the World Social Forum the idea of "globalization from below" has become immensely popular. Yet, in many counter movements that oppose corporate globalization, global visions about alternative futures continue to be generated and disseminated from above to people who are working to define for themselves their local struggles and their interconnections with processes at other levels. An assumption often made by anti-corporate globalization activists is that since local struggles are often not connected in obvious ways, activists who operate at the very local scale cannot make linkages beyond the local.[22] But the processes by which political struggles and visions develop are highly uneven, and real and tangible connections between those struggles need to be explored and cultivated. Visionaries who wish to see critiques of global processes articulated in local struggles may need to refocus their attention and energies on the ways in which place-based struggles might be facilitated and supported, and to identify the varied processes of struggle out of which alternative visions would emerge. There are no models to do this but Sangtin Yatra provides one example of an intellectual and political team effort, the terms and agendas of which are not predetermined or imposed. Through a collective journey, the authors come to articulate political critiques that overlap with those developed by anti-corporate globalization activists. But this one emerges in a more organic fashion.

Ironically, while the anti-corporate globalization activists bemoan the lack of a global vision in locally defined struggles, the articulation of any politics that is global in scope becomes easily suspect in some feminist circles. Much of the suspicion is rooted in the important debate over "global sisterhood," an idea that has been variously approached, problematized, critiqued and revisited.[23] But precisely because global sisterhood has inspired the emergence of a UN-style global feminist agenda, critics of global sisterhood also have a responsibility to engage with global feminism and imagine new forms of feminist solidarity across borders.[24] *Sangtin Yatra/Playing with Fire* suggests that collaborative praxes that engage with place-based specificities of local processes and struggles can help us articulate transnational feminist alternatives to "global sisterhood" and "global feminisms." The collective's critiques of empowerment, its approach to such questions as seclusion, veiling and negotiation of salaries in the autobiographers' own households, as well as the admittedly limited engagement of the activists with questions of same-sex sexuality, challenge the feminist intellectual in the northern (wherever that north might be geographically situated) academy to immerse herself in the complex and contradictory realities of the activists' milieu. To confront such a challenge she must try to understand the autobiographers' analysis from their location; she must ask why theoretical frameworks that she might consider "cutting-edge" do not adequately speak to or resonate with the activists' understandings and conceptualizations; she must be prepared to acknowledge the limits of the discourses that she might be inserted in and to orchestrate shifts in them in ways that can become meaningful for her transnational critics and collaborators.

Sangtin Yatra as Transnational Feminist Border-crossing

As processes and effects of globalization and neo-liberalism have become central to the agendas of progressive academics, questions surrounding critical praxis, reflexive activism, and relevant theory have acquired renewed momentum and urgency. For at least two decades now, feminist theorists from various philosophical locations have reflected on the relationships among decolonization, anticapitalist critique, oppositional practices and emancipatory education,[25] and several excellent examples have emerged of the ways in which ethics and the politics of solidarity can be enacted "on the ground" and across borders.[26] These engagements and interventions have clearly established the importance of interweaving theory and praxis in feminist work. At the same time, however, the persistence of the traditional compartmentalization of theory and methodology has often prevented academics working across borders from engaging more centrally with theory *as* praxis,[27] and from focusing more explicitly on the questions of socio-political relevance in knowledge production.[28] Peake and Trotz explicitly pose the question of how Third World and First World women can work together "in ways that are authorized by dialogue with [Third World subjects] and not just First World audiences." Reflexive questioning of ourselves and of the techniques we use to develop multivocality, they remind us, must be accompanied by a continued interrogation of how our supposedly "improved" representational strategies might be constituting new silences.[29] Such an interrogation requires that we tap into the tremendous potential of activism, and produce critical analyses based on local feminist praxis, and the ways that such praxis connects with broader relations of domination and subordination.[30]

This journey of *sangtins* suggests that our engagements with local feminist praxis hinge, in important ways, on our ability to imagine new forms of border-crossings and "translations" through which transnational collaborators can enact shifts in prevailing practices of knowledge production—that is, shifts in dominant expectations about (a) which actors can produce knowledge, (b) the methodology and content of knowledges produced, (c) the languages, genres and forms in which knowledges get produced, (d) and the manner in which new knowledges gain relevance as they reach different audiences and enable new kinds of socio-political interventions. Below, I consider some of the ways in which *Sangtin Yatra/Playing with Fire* makes a conscious attempt to enact these four shifts.

As gender politics become increasingly professionalized and controlled by formally educated and urban based "gender experts" and "trainers," terms such as "field site," "research project," "case studies," and "life histories" no longer remain confined primarily to the domain(s) of elite northern academics who temporarily relocate themselves to southern locations. Actors located at multiple scales in the NGO hierarchy (e.g., national-level supervisors, state-level programme directors, district-level project coordinators, village-level mobilizers, etc.) have come to play significant roles in the contested realm of formal knowledge production. Questions of voice, power, privilege and subalternity have acquired new dimensions and complexities in this new socio-political scenario.[31]

Sangtin Yatra/Playing with Fire recognizes the ways in which socio-spatial embeddedness of village-level activists places them in a unique position to analyze the multiple webs of power in which their everyday lives, struggles and aspirations are inserted.

The collaboration with the activists gives me a critical medium to engage with politics on the "ground" through a collective process of agenda formation and analysis. At the same time, the process allows all of us to advance our understandings—in this case, by placing issues such as "politics of knowledge production" and "NGOization of women's empowerment" at the core of our intellectual agendas and frameworks. In this way, we begin to blur the divide between academia, activism and NGO fields; develop multi-layered understandings of the contextually embedded processes, struggles and actors involved in the discourse, praxis and politics of "empowerment;" and facilitate the creation of new spaces and frameworks for public debate.

Although NGOs in the global south have become a focal point of vigorous debate, perspectives of community-based NGO activists who mobilize people on the ground have, for the most part, been absent from these debates. The journey of *sangtins* shows how the process of imagining and enacting a collaboration can open new spaces for NGO actors and academics to address how local patriarchies intersect with complex layers of casteism, communalism, classism and global capitalism, and to raise sensitive issues of elitism, casteism and professionalization in NGO-led empowerment. Neither academics nor NGO workers, as isolated entities, can easily obtain institutional or political support to address these issues. We believe that the things we were able to say in the book would have gone unheard in the NGO circles if we had authored the same analyses as isolated individuals. Our collective voice allowed us not only to explore how we could produce new forms of knowledge, but also to gain a space and legitimacy for our critique and reflections that we would not have found in the absence of the specific kind of transnational alliance that we created. For example, the issues of inequity and lack of transparency that the activists had been raising in their organizational meetings for the last five years had been continuously dismissed on the grounds that their expectations were unrealistic. Conversely, if I had solely authored this work as an academic piece with "voices" of the activists incorporated in it, it would have either gone unnoticed in the NGO circles of Uttar Pradesh or my critique of NGOization would have been marginalized as the inaccessible musings of a distant academic located in the ivory towers of a northern institution. Our coming together from a diverse set of social, geographical and institutional locations, however, allowed us to craft an intellectual agenda and methodology that allowed all of us to develop our understandings of globalization, development, geographies of difference and scale, and to grapple with how these could be used to re-imagine concrete place-based politics. With respect to the ways in which links between the global and the local can serve to bypass state elites, it is also critical to note that when our ability to work collectively was threatened by the attacks from NSY, Uttar Pradesh, it was the political pressure created by a transnational cyber petition that stopped further harassment of the autobiographers.

Far from simply generating an interlinked collection of seven autobiographies, then, Sangtin Yatra became a vehicle to analyze a range of broader processes at work – including the ways in which hierarchical processes within NGOs can impede their stated goal of empowerment – as well as a journey through which the activists became deeply engaged in changing their world and envisioning their own future. This process has provided a concrete space to not only "learn from below" but to also determine the specific ways in which each of us can learn to be accountable to people's struggles for self-representation and self-determination.

In an era of global mediation, the significance of languages cannot be underestimated in any political discussion of knowledge production. Indeed, the discursive divides between the spaces of the "vernacular" and the spaces of "elite languages" have never been so critical in defining the landscapes of survival and struggle.[32] These gaps have provided the locus for articulating many movement-based critiques of uneven development and disenfranchisement caused by globalization. The politics of language have, in fact, fuelled and enabled each phase of this collaboration. From the outset, the autobiographers instinctively understood that a desire to intervene in the realm of knowledge production implied that they would have to write their narratives in Hindi, even if Awadhi was the language in which they reflected on their personal lives and collective issues. Yet, in the book,

Sangtin Yatra, we tried to Awadhi-*ize* our reflections when possible in order to remind the readers that literacy and writing – as well as the linguistic medium in which they happen – can never be separated from the politics of (dis)empowerment and uneven development. In the socio-political context of the "Hindi belt" where communal fissures between Hindus and Muslims are often sharpened by splitting Urdu apart from Hindi, *Sangtin Yatra*, furthermore, resisted the definitions and constraints of "pure" Hindi or Urdu by tapping into the richness and power of both of these artificially compartmentalized languages.

Alongside languages, *Sangtin Yatra* and *Playing with Fire* also muddies the idea of "pure" genres by interspersing reflections, conversations, excerpts from diaries letters and petitions with what is regarded as an academic-style of writing. By recognizing that the politics of language and genres is central to a project that focuses on social exclusion and elitism and by continuously grappling with this issue in our praxis, our effort sought to destabilize the boundaries among academic/non-academic, theory/praxis, vernacular/English, as well as between theoretical, creative and activist writings. Rather than producing knowledges in different genres for different audiences, this blurring of genres and languages in one product allowed *Sangtin Yatra* to speak simultaneously to different audiences in rural and urban centres of the Hindi belt; to spark conversations in the Hindi media in Lucknow, Kanpur, Allahabad, Patna, New Delhi and Kolkata; in the office spaces of the NGOs in Uttar Pradesh; and in the homes and communities of NGO workers. Furthermore, within a week of its public release, the collective was being asked to consider translating *Sangtin Yatra* into English for a nation-wide audience, and into Urdu, Marathi and Bengali for audiences in other "vernacular" spaces of the country. This need for translation, especially into English, became more urgent as the authors became targets of attack, and as we had to move in the global cyber space with our petition to stop those attacks. Rather than moving from the global or national English media, then, the conversations and controversies generated by *Sangtin Yatra* moved from the local and regional spaces of Awadhi and Hindi into the national and global spaces of English. Each "translation" allowed the stories and critiques of this journey to reach new audiences and enable new kinds of discussions on questions of NGOization as well as intellectual practice and politics.

The process, products, controversies and alliances emerging from this journey have found multiple textual forms—books, newspaper articles, reviews, a petition, resignation letters, and more diary writing.[33] The inclusion of some of these texts in *Playing with Fire* is an extension of the idea that knowledge grows out of, and is embodied in, dialogue. Each dialogue has allowed the production of new knowledges that can become usable and relevant for us and for the audiences we want to reach. The text of *Playing with Fire* does not so much document or reflect the theory and praxis of collaboration as it enacts them. Theory of collaboration is generated *as* praxis; that is, what matters in this intellectual and political journey is not just theory-as-product but also the activity of knowledge production, especially as a site for negotiating difference and power. Through processes of negotiation and struggle within and beyond the collective, varied knowledges evolving in specific places and institutions interact with each other to produce new forms of knowledge. In other words, what is significant about this journey is not simply what the *sangtins* are in a position to see or theorize – it is about what we are in a position to do in producing knowledge – namely, constitute ourselves as political actors in institutions and processes both near and far. The usefulness or effectiveness of *Playing with Fire*, then, cannot be assessed in terms of whether it accurately or authentically represents the *sangtins* to the readers, but on the basis of whether and how it can become a part of the authors' individual and collective agency; and serve the critical activism out of which this book evolved.

With every new knowledge, however, also come the risks of that knowledge being appropriated in unintended forms and unforeseen spaces by institutions and individuals. Even as we brace ourselves to face these risks, we believe that our collaboration thus far has given the activists the tools to resist the donor-driven forms of empowerment and to articulate an alternative framework for imagining and enacting globalization from below. In addition to triggering many important conversations about authority and "truth telling," *Sangtin Yatra* and its effects are drawing attention to the very issues that have been simmering in women's NGOs throughout India but that have largely remained invisible in formal reports and analyses.

At the same time, the collective achingly recognizes that the seven autobiographers' bold decision to come out as authors of their own insights and critiques from within the margins of their institution has pushed us into a long-term battle for the survival of the very dream that this *yatra* has come to express—the dream of nurturing an alternative vision of social change in a place that is hijacked by the mainstream models of donor-driven empowerment. The biggest challenge that the *sangtins* now face is to create the spaces to expand and grow in the directions where our political critiques are leading us.

As long as that challenge remains, SangtinYatra will continue.

Notes

[1] The transfer orders targeted Richa Singh and individuals who were seen as allies of the authors. For the seven authors employed in NSY on monthly honoraria (ranging from Rs. 800 to Rs. 10,000) without any forms of insurance, pension or job security, the threats of disciplinary action in five cases came in the absence of any contract that defined the parameters or responsibilities associated with their employment in NSY. In two cases, where the workers had contracts, there was nothing in the contract to prevent them from writing about their work in the field.

[2] In addition to the articles noted in notes 21 and 22 of Introduction, news reports about the book release and book excerpts appeared in the following Hindi dailies: *Hindustan* (Lucknow) March 21 2004, 4; March 25 2004, 5; March 26 2004, 11; *Rashtriya Sahara* (Lucknow) March 26 2004, 5; *Dainik Jagran* (Lucknow) March 26 2004, 4; *Jansatta Express* (Lucknow) March 26 2004, 2; *Sahara Samaya Samagra* (Sunday magazine, New Delhi) April 10 2004, 21. Book reviews in Hindi periodicals not listed in Introduction include: Kshama Sharma, "Aao Sakhi Chalen Sang-Sang," *Kadambini* July 2004, 181-182; Krishna Kumar, "Striyon ke Shabd," *Jan Satta* July 11 2004, 2; Devendra Chowbey, "Anubhav ke Sach," *India Today* August 2 2004, 54-56; Medha, "Stree ke Niji Anubhavon se Bhare Sach," *Hindustan*, Ravi Utsav August 8 2004, 2; Janmat, "Sangtin Yatra," *Janmat* 23:2-3 (2004), 119-122; K. B. Singh, "Aansuon se Aashaon tak phaila Nari Sansar," *Vishwa Patrakar Sadan* 4:15 (2004), 48-53; Kamal Kumar, "Zameeni Sachchaiyon se jura Stree Vimarsh," *Naya Gyanodaya* 26, April 2005, 132-133.

[3] This petition signed by scholars and NGO-based activists from India, Nepal, the UK and the USA was mailed from Minneapolis on June 18, 2004 to seven departments and ministries of the Governments of India and U.P. that pertained to education, literacy, human resources and development. The explicit attacks on the autobiographers stopped soon after this petition reached Lucknow and New Delhi, but it did not result in the revocation of Richa Singh's punitive transfer.

[4] Amy Kaminsky, the chair of Women's Studies at Minnesota, wrote a response (June 19, 2004) to the Director of NSY, U.P., supporting *Sangtin Yatra* and arguing that the nine authors of *Sangtin Yatra* were protected by the doctrine of academic freedom, and by the constitutional rights to free speech and expression unconstrained by the agendas of others. She expressed concern that the collaborators would be punished, and pointed out that the more important thing was not whether the activists wrote the book as employees of NSY or members of Sangtin, but that the work they did actually took place. It should be noted that the State Programme Director of NSY, U.P. who spearheaded the backlash against the authors of *Sangtin Yatra*, resigned from NSY, U.P. in April, 2005, as the manuscript of *Playing with Fire* was going into production.

[5] Richa Singh disagrees with this interpretation.

[6] Dated 31 May, 2004; Translated from Hindi.

[7] Dated 22 April, 2004; Translated from Hindi.

[8] The discussion in Chapter One of the risks that the authors had taken (especially, the story about Chaandni's and Radha's husbands reading their diaries) was interpreted by NSY, U.P., as a sign of the irresponsibility of both Richas, who placed the writers in jeopardy in their own homes. NSY, U.P., failed to appreciate the autobiographers as authors who had chosen to take these risks on their own.

[9] Krishna Kumar, "Striyon ke Shabd." Translated from Hindi. Krishna Kumar is Professor of Education at the University of Delhi, and the Director of National Council of Educational Research and Training.

[10] Krishna Kumar, "Village Voices: Positive Trends in Education in UP," *The Times of India* (English daily, New Delhi) August 6, 2004. Downloaded August 7, 2004 from: http://timesofindia.indiatimes.com/articleshow/804426.cms

[11] Krishna Kumar, "Striyon ke Shabd." Krishna Kumar points out that the *sangtins*' reflections of childhood suggest why the rural girl-child has been such a source of frustration for the government and UNESCO that only one out of a hundred is able to make her way to the grade twelve examination.

[12] For a complex discussion of feminisms and practices such as "veiling" in relation to the politics of class and the projects of "modernization" see, Lila Abu-Lughod, "Feminist Longings and Postcolonial Conditions," in

Remaking Women: Feminism and Modernity in the Middle East, ed. Lila Abu-Lughod, (Princeton: Princeton University Press, 1998) 1-31.

[13] See, for example, Leela Fernandes, *Producing Workers: The Politics of Gender, Class and Culture in the Calcutta Jute Mills* (Philadelphia: University of Pennsylvania Press, 1997).

[14] Krishna Kumar, "Striyon ke Shabd." Translated from Hindi.

[15] Chachage, "The World Social Forum," 18-19.

[16] See also, Roy, "Tide? Or Ivory Snow?"

[17] David Hulme and Michael Edwards, "NGOs, States and Donors: An Overview," in *NGOs, States and Donors: Too Close for Comfort?,* eds. David Hulme and Michael Edwards (London: Macmillan Press Ltd, 1997), 3.

[18] David Lewis and Tina Wallace, "Introduction," in *New Roles and Relevance: Development NGOs and the Challenge of Change,* eds. David Lewis and Tina Wallace (Bloomfield, CT: Kumarian Press, 2000) xiv.

[19] Kamat, *Development Hegemony* 3.

[20] Gayatri Chakravorty Spivak, "Discussion: An Afterword on the New Subaltern," in *Subaltern Studies XI: Community, Gender, and Violence,* eds. Partha Chatterjee and Pradeep Jeganathan (Delhi: Permanent Black and New Delhi: Ravi Dayal Publisher, 2000) 319.

[21] Gayatri Chakravorty Spivak, "Discussion: An Afterword on the New Subaltern," 325. Koni Benson and Richa Nagar, "Collaboration as Resistance: Reconsidering Processes, Products and Possibilities of Feminist Oral History and Ethnography", *Gender, Place and Culture,* Forthcoming.

[22] These assumptions are reflected, for instance, in the work of Jeremy Brecher who acknowledges the importance of creating and strengthening "self-defining grassroots organizations of the disempowered" while at the same time urging "social movement activists" "to define the goals of such groups in ways that are congruent with the common interests of people and planet." See, Jeremy Brecher, "The Hierarchs' New World Order—and Ours," in *Global Visions: Beyond the New World Order,* eds., Jeremy Brecher, John Brown Childs, and Jill Cutler (Boston: South End Press,1993) 11. Others, however, challenge such a global vision. For example, Notes from Nowhere, *We are Everywhere: The Irresistible Rise of Global Anticapitalism* (London: Verso, 2003) 506 argue against "a new ideology to impose from above, to 'replace' capitalism, but evolving a new, radically participatory methodology from below." These authors (506) "rather than seeking a map to tomorrow," emphasize "developing our own journeys, individually and collectively, as we travel." For a nuanced analysis of the complexities involved in processes by which local groups "jump scales" in their efforts to contest the power of global capital, see Jim Glassman, "From Seattle (and Ubon) to Bangkok: The Scales of Resistance to Corporate Globalization," *Environment and*

Planning D: Society and Space, 2001, 513-533. Also see, Michael Hardt, "Today's Bandung?" *New Left Review* 14 (March-April) 2002, 112-118.

[23] Chandra Talpade Mohanty provides an excellent critique of Robin Morgan's (1984) *Sisterhood is Global* in her essay, "Sisterhood, Coalition and the Politics of Experience" in Chandra Talpade Mohanty, 2003, *Feminism Without Borders: Decolonizing Theory, Practicing Solidarity* (Durham: Duke University Press, 2003), 106-123. Also, see Amrita Basu's "Introduction," in *The Challenge of Local Feminisms: Women's Movements in Global Perspective,* ed. Amrita Basu (Boulder: Westview Press, 1995), 1-21.

[24] See Chandra Talpade Mohanty, "Under Western Eyes Revisited: Solidarity through Anti-capitalist struggles," in *Feminism Without Borders,* 221-251.

[25] See, for example, M. Jacqui Alexander and Chandra Talpade Mohanty, eds., *Feminist Genealogies, Colonial Legacies, Democratic Futures* (New York: Routledge, 1997); Mohanty, *Feminism Without Borders;* Torres, *Chicana Without Apology.* Gibson-Graham approach such issues in terms of "post-modern feminist social research" (See J. K. Gibson-Graham, "Stuffed if I know! Reflections on Post-Modern Feminist Social Research," *Gender, Place and Culture* 1:2 (1994), 205-224) whereas Grewal and Kaplan approach them in terms of problematizing feminist theory (Inderpal Grewal and Caren Kaplan, "Introduction: Transnational Feminist Practices and Questions of Postmodernity," in *Scattered Hegemonies: Postmodernity and Transnational Feminist Practices,* eds. Inderpal Grewal and Caren Kaplan (Minneapolis: University of Minnesota Press, 1994) 1-33.

[26] Rigoberta Menchú, *I, Rigoberta Menchú: An Indian Woman in Guatemala,* edited and introduced by Elisabeth Burgos-Debray; translated by Ann Wright (London: Verso, 1984); Stree Shakti Sanghatana, *We were Making History: Women and the Telangana Uprising* (New Delhi: Kali for Women, 1989); Women's Research and Development Project, *Unsung Heroines* (Dar es Salaam: WRDP, 1991); Janet Silman, ed., *Enough is Enough: Aboriginal Women Speak Out,* (Toronto: The Women's Press, 1987).

[27] I use the terms, "theory," "praxis" and "methodology" here in the sense used by Pamela Moss, "Taking on, Thinking About, and Doing Feminist Research in Geography," in *Feminist Geography in Practice: Research and Methods,* ed. Pamela Moss (Oxford: Blackwell, 2002), 1-17. Moss (12-13) defines "theory" as "a combination of both conceptualizations of phenomena and an explanation of how phenomena work, exist or articulate;" for her "praxis" is "a politically active way to live in the world" while feminist methodology is "about the approach to research, including the conventional aspects of research – the design, the data collection, the analysis, and the circulation of information – and

the lesser acknowledged aspects of conventional research – relationships among people involved in the research process, the actual conduct of the research, and process through which the research comes to be undertaken and completed."

[28] Appadurai argues that academic knowledge production, particularly in the US, has contributed to the creation of a form of "apartheid" and notes how the production of academic/global "experts" is based on a denial of epistemic significance to "vernacular" knowledges. See, Arjun Appadurai, "Grassroots Globalization and the Research Imagination," *Public Culture* 12:1 (2000): 1-19 and Obioma Nnaemeka, "Nego-Feminism: Theorizing, Practicing and Pruning Africa's Way," *Signs* 29:2 (2004): 357-385. As a way to address the "increasing divorce between the parochial debates . . . in the academy on the one hand and the vernacular discourses and realities of constituencies outside the academy on the other hand," Nnaemeka (360) urges us to look for the "third space of engagement." This third space "is not the either/ or location of stability; it is the both/ and space where borderless territory and free movement authorize the capacity to simultaneously theorize practice, practice theory, and allow the mediations of policy." From their specific location in Indian feminist movements, Kannabiran and Kannabiran (279) also raise critical questions about the politics and assumptions of global feminism and their relationship with "our own assumptions as feminists in the Third World." See, Vasanth Kannabiran and Kalpana Kannabiran, "Looking at Ourselves: The Women's Movement in Hyderabad," in eds. Alexander and Mohanty, *Feminist Genealogies, Colonial Legacies, Democratic Futures* (New York: Routledge, 1997), 259-279.

Others who have variously approached the notion of relevance with reference to the purposes and effects of scholarly knowledge production, include: Syed Farid Alatas, "The Study of the Social Sciences in Developing Societies: Towards an Adequate Conceptualization of Relevance," *Current Sociology* 49:2 (2001): 1-19; Jean Dreze, "On Research and Activism," *Economic and Political Weekly* 37:9 (2002): 817; Ellen Messer-Davidow *Disciplining Feminisms* (Durham: Duke University Press, 2002); Ellen Messer-Davidow, "Feminist Studies and Social Activism," Paper presented at the Feminist Studies Colloquium Series, Department of Women's Studies, University of Minnesota, Minneapolis, September 30, 2002; Guy Poitevin, *The Voice and the Will: Subaltern Agency: Forms and Motives* (New Delhi: Manohar, 2002); Ramachandra Guha, "The Ones Who Stayed Behind," *Economic and Political Weekly*, 38:11-12 (2003): 1121-1124; Richa Nagar, "Footloose researchers, Traveling Theories and the Politics of Transnational Feminist Praxis;" Geraldine Pratt, *Working Feminisms* (Philadelphia: Temple University Press, 2004).

[29] Linda Peake and D. Alison Trotz, *Gender, Place and Ethnicity* (New York: Routledge, 1999) 28, 35.

[30] Linda Peake and Audrey Kobayashi, "Policies and Practices for an Anti-racist Geography at the Millennium," *The Professional Geographer* 54:1 (2002): 50-61; Linda Peake and D. Alison Trotz, "Feminism and Feminist Issues in the South," in *The Companion to Development Studies*, eds. V. Desai and R.B. Potter (London: Arnold, 2001) 34-37.

[31] See, Lazreg, "Development"; Nnaemeka, "Nego-Feminism"; Appadurai, "Grassroots Globalization and the Research Imagination"; Benson and Nagar, "Collaboration as Resistance."

[32] Krishna Kumar, *Raj, Samaj aur Shiksha* (New Delhi: Rajkamal Prakashan, 1990). Krishna Kumar, *Political Agenda of Education: A Study of Colonialist and Nationalist Ideas*, New Delhi: Sage Publications, 1991); David Faust and Richa Nagar, "English Medium Education, Social Fracturing, and the Politics of Development in Postcolonial India," *Economic and Political Weekly*, 36:30 (2001): 2878-2883; Appadurai, "Grassroots Globalization and the Research Imagination."

[33] Five out of nine *sangtins* have continued to write diaries, and a newsletter in Hindi called *Sangtin Yatra Jaari Hai* (Sangtin Yatra continues...) is being planned by old and new members of Sangtin, which on the basis of ongoing reflections and struggles, seeks to share notes with readers near and far about Sangtin's evolving journeys on issues raised in the original *Sangtin Yatra*.

Glossary

aabroo (see also, *izzat aabroo*)—social prestige, honour, respectability.

aanchal (see also, *palloo*)—the loose end of a woman's *sari* that covers her chest and may or may not be pulled over the head.

Aanganwadi—village preschools, funded by the government.

abha—light, splendour.

Abba/Abbu—father.

agni pareeksha—trial by fire—associated with the legend of Rama's wife, Sita, when her loyalty was to be tested after she was abducted by Ravana (the "demon") and won back by Rama (the "God").

Baba (see also, *Dada*)—paternal grandfather.

Babu, Babuji, Babul (also, *Pitaji*)—father.

Bahu—daughter-in-law.

Bahanji—Female school-teacher.

barat—wedding procession that accompanies the groom.

beegha—a measure for land (1 *beegha* = 27,200 square feet).

Beti (also, *bitiya*)—daughter.

Bhabhi—sister-in-law (brother's wife).

Bhaiyya—brother.

Bhangi—a Dalit caste, traditionally assigned the task of sweeping, cleaning, scavenging and disposing of human waste.

bidai—the ceremony when the bride is sent off from her parents' home (*mayaka*) to her parents'-in-law home (*sasural*).

bidi—cigarettes rolled by hand in leaves.

Block—administrative subdivision comprising a cluster of villages within a district.

Bua—father's sister.

chadar (also, *chador, chaddar*)—a covering or shawl (longer, heavier, and wider than a *dupatta*) that is used by upper caste daughters-in-law to symbolize the "more respectable" status of their families.

Chamar—a term (considered derogatory) for *Raidas* caste, traditionally associated with the work involving animal hides, shoemaking and tannery.
charge-sheets—written accusations.
chatai—straw-mat.
chikankari—an art of embroidery for which Lucknow is famous.
crore—one crore is equal to ten million.
Dadi—paternal grandmother.
dari—rug.
Devar—brother-in-law (husband's younger brother).
Dhankun—a Dalit caste, whose women cut the umbilical cords of new borns.
Didi—older sister.
district—administrative subdivision of a state or province.
doli—palinquin in which the bride is taken from her parents' home to her parents'-in-law home.
Dwarchar—the ceremony to welcome the groom and the wedding procession that accompanies him.
field—In the NGO parlance, *field* denotes the geographical area that is the focus of a program's activities.
ghee—clarified butter.
Gudiya—a monsoon festival observed in the Sitapur district. During this festival, girls and women make rag dolls (*gudiya*) and bring them to a public place, where their brothers thrash the dolls with a whip.
gur—jaggery.
ghoonghat—the end of a woman's *sari* that is placed over the head and is pulled down to cover the face.
ghughri—a snack made of spiced lentils (*chana*).
haraam—unlawful, prohibited.
havan—a Hindu religious ceremony in which sacrificial offerings to God are made through the medium of fire.
Hindi-belt—term used to denote the strip of states in Northern India where Hindi is the dominant language. The states include but are not confined to Bihar, Madhya Pradesh, Rajasthan, Uttar Pradesh and Uttranchal.
Hindutva—Hindu-supremacist ideology.
Intermediate—twelfth grade.
Jeth—husband's older brother.
Jhansi ki Rani—Lakshmibai, the queen of Jhansi, who fought in the war for Indian independence against the British in 1857 and is known for her bravery.
Jija—older sister's husband.
kaajal—kohl used to decorate the eyes.
kachori—a deep-fried pastry stuffed with lentils.

Kaleva—breakfast; here used for ceremonial breakfast after the wedding.
kanya—unmarried girl.
karamjali—literally, burned fate; a term of abuse.
khandani—of the extended family, of the clan.
Khadi boli—generally used to indicate the formal Hindi/Hindustani language that is spoken chiefly in the urban areas of several North Indian states, including Uttar Pradesh. It is often deployed to highlight the contrast between the formal, written Hindi (generally associated with the urban areas), and the informal, spoken "dialects" of the rural areas (referred to somewhat degradingly, as *dehati*—or, of the village).
Khuda—Allah, God.
kuchcha—mud and thatch; unbaked.
kuleen—reputed.
Kurmi—classified as an "Other Backward Caste."
Mama/Mamu—mother's brother.
Mandir-Masjid debate—the dispute over the Babri Mosque and Ramjanmabhoomi in Ayodhya.
Masi/Mausi—mother's sister.
Maurya—classified as an "Other Backward Caste."
Mausa/Mausia—husband of mother's sister.
med—boundary of the farm.
mithai—sweets.
naak—literally, nose. Symbolic of prestige.
Nagpanchmi—A festival observed during the monsoon and marked by the worshipping of the *Naag* or serpent.
Naimisharanya—A famous holy place of Hindu pilgrimage located in Sitapur District.
Nana—maternal grandfather.
Nanad—sister-in-law.
Nani—maternal grandmother.
naqab—mask, veil, or hood. Used synonymously with *burqa*.
Navratri—the festival of nine nights when the Goddess Durga is worshipped.
nikah—wedding.
OBCs/*Other Backward Castes*—Neither Sawarn nor Dalit, these castes are ranked above castes that are officially classified as "scheduled."
Paasi—a Dalit caste, considered higher than Raidas.
Pachcho—Sandhya's nickname "*Pachcho*"came from the Hindi word, *paanch* (meaning, five), since she was a sister of five brothers.
Panchayat—village court or arbitrating body.
Pathan—a Sunni Muslim community that traces its origins to North West Pakistan and Afghanistan. Considered as "upper-caste" among Sunnis.
Phoophi (see also, *Bua*)—father's sister.

prasad—food offered to Hindu Gods and distributed to devotees after *pooja*.
purva—neighborhood, settlement.
rab—a thick substance made out of cooked sugarcane juice.
Ramleela—folk theatre about the life of Rama, based on Ramayana. The actors are usually amateur and come from the localities where the performances take place.
Ravana—the "demon" from Ramayana, who abducted Rama's wife, Sita.
reservation policies—affirmative action policies intended to correct the injustices against members of the underprivileged castes and "tribes."
Saas—mother-in-law.
Saavan—a monsoon month in the Hindu calendar that overlaps with the month of July.
sabzi—vegetables.
Samdhi—father-in-law of daughter or son.
Samdhin—mother-in-law of daughter or son.
samlaingikta—same-sex sexuality.
sandhya—evening.
Sasur—father-in-law.
Sasuralwala—person from the *sasural*.
Sawarn—Elite Hindu castes of Brahman, Kshatriya and Vaishya.
scheduled castes—official classification of the Dalit castes.
seela—the grain that is left behind in the field after the harvest.
Shagun—a custom observed in Sitapur at the time of wedding, in which the groom symbolically hits the bride with a stick. Literally, it means, good omen.
Shraddh—offerings made by a family to the souls of its dead so that they may rest in peace.
sutiya—an ornament of the neck.
Taiji—wife of father's older brother.
talaaq—divorce.
Tauji—father's older brother.
tempo—a three-wheeled motorized public transportation.
tilak—engagement ceremony.
toti wala lota—a small pitcher with a spout.
totka—a kind of supernatural practice associated with witchcraft.
tulsi—basil plant, considered auspicious by Hindus.
Ustani—term used in Chaandni's school for Muslim female teacher.
zarda—in this context, sweetened saffron-coloured rice.

Select Bibliography

Abu-Lughod, Lila (1998), "Feminist Longings and Postcolonial Conditions," In *Remaking Women: Feminism and Modernity in the Middle East*, ed. Lila Abu-Lughod, 1-31, Princeton: Princeton University Press.

Agarwal, Bina (1994), "Gender and Command Over Property: A Critical Gap in Economic Analysis and Policy in South Asia," *World Development* 22:10: 1455-1478.

Alatas, Syed Farid (2001), "The Study of the Social Sciences in Developing Societies: Towards an Adequate Conceptualization of Relevance," *Current Sociology* 49:2: 1-19.

Alexander, M. Jacqui and Chandra Talpade Mohanty, eds. (1997), *Feminist Genealogies, Colonial Legacies, Democratic Futures*, New York: Routledge.

Anupamlata, et al. (2004), *Sangtin Yatra: Sat Zindagiyon Mein Lipta Nari Vimarsh*, Sitapur: Sangtin.

Appadurai, Arjun (2000), "Grassroots Globalization and the Research Imagination," *Public Culture* 12:1: 1-19.

Basu, Amrita (1995), "Introduction," In *The Challenge of Local Feminisms: Women's Movements in Global Perspective*, ed. Amrita Basu, 1-21, Boulder: Westview Press.

Benson, Koni and Richa Nagar, "Collaboration as Resistance: Reconsidering Processes, Products and Possibilities of Feminist Oral History and Ethnography," *Gender, Place and Culture*, Forthcoming.

Brecher, Jeremy (1993), "The Hierarchs' New World Order—and Ours," In *Global Visions: Beyond the New World Order*, eds. Jeremy Brecher, John Brown Childs, and Jill Cutler, 3-12, Boston: South End Press.

Chachage, Seithy L. Chachage (2004), "The World Social Forum: Lessons from Mumbai," Manuscript, Published in six installments in *The African* [English daily, Dar es Salaam] February 23-38, 31 pp.

Debroy, Bibek and Laveesh Bhandari, eds. (2003), *District-level Deprivation in the New Millennium*, New Delhi: Konark Publishers.

Dreze, Jean (2002), "On Research and Activism," *Economic and Political Weekly* 37:9: 817.

Faust, David and Richa Nagar (2001), "English Medium Education, Social Fracturing, and the Politics of Development in Postcolonial India," *Economic and Political Weekly* 36:30: 2878-2883.

Fernandes, Leela (1997), *Producing Workers: The Politics of Gender, Class and Culture in the Calcutta Jute Mills*, Philadelphia: University of Pennsylvania Press.

Freire, Paulo (1993), *Pedagogy of the Oppressed*, New York: The Continuum Publishing Company.

Gibson-Graham, J. K. (1994), "Stuffed if I know! Reflections on Post-modern Feminist Social Research," *Gender, Place and Culture* 1:2: 205-224.

Glassman, Jim (2001), "From Seattle (and Ubon) to Bangkok: The Scales of Resistance to Corporate Globalization," *Environment and Planning D: Society and Space* 513-533.

Grewal, Inderpal and Caren Kaplan (1994), "Introduction: Transnational Feminist Practices and Questions of Postmodernity," In *Scattered Hegemonies: Postmodernity and Transnational Feminist Practices*, eds. Inderpal Grewal and Caren Kaplan, 1-33, Minneapolis: University of Minnesota Press.

Guha, Ramachandra (2003), "The Ones Who Stayed Behind," *Economic and Political Weekly* 38:11-12: 1121-1124.

Hardt, Michael (2002), "Today's Bandung"? *New Left Review* 14: 112-118.

Hulme, David and Michael Edwards (1997), "NGOs, States and Donors: An Overview." In *NGOs, States and Donors: Too Close for Comfort?* eds. David Hulme and Michael Edwards, 3-22, London: Macmillan Press Ltd in association with Save the Children.

John, Mary E. (2002), "Feminism, Poverty and Globalization: An Indian View," *Inter-Asia Cultural Studies* 3:3: 351-367.

Kamat, Sangeeta (2002), *Development Hegemony: NGOs and the State in India*, New Delhi: Oxford University Press.

Kannabiran, Vasanth and Kalpana Kannabiran (1997), "Looking at Ourselves: The Women's Movement in Hyderabad," In *Feminist Genealogies, Colonial Legacies, Democratic Futures*, eds. M. Jacqui Alexander and Chandra Talpade Mohanty, 259-279, New York: Routledge.

Kumar, Krishna (1990), *Raj, Samaj aur Shiksha*, New Delhi: Rajkamal Prakashan.

—— (1991), *Political Agenda of Education: A Study of Colonialist and Nationalist Ideas*, New Delhi: Sage.

—— (2004), "Striyon ke Shabd," *Jan Satta* [Hindi Daily, New Delhi] Jul 11: 2.

—— (2004), "Village Voices: Positive Trends in Education in U.P.," *The Times of India* [English Daily] August 6, 2004. Downloaded August 7, 2004 from: http://timesofindia.indiatimes.com/articleshow/804426.cms

Kumar, Radha (1993), *The History of Doing: An Illustrated Account of Movements for Women's Rights and Feminism in India, 1800-1990*, New Delhi: Kali for Women.

Kushawarti, Bandhu (2004), "Saat Zindagiyon Mein Lipta Nari Vimarsh," *Aakhir Kab Tak?* [Hindi periodical, Lucknow] 2:6: 25-26.

Lang, Sabine (2002), "The NGO-ization of Feminism: Institutionalization and Institution Building Within the German Women's Movement," In *Global Feminisms Since 1945*, ed. Bonnie Smith, 290-304, New York: Routledge.

Lazreg, Marnia (2002), "Development: Feminist Theory's Cul-de-sac." In *Feminist Postdevelopment Thought: Rethinking Modernity, Postcolonialism, Representation*, ed. Kriemild Saunders, 123-145, London: Zed.

Lewis, David and Tina Wallace (2000), "Introduction," In *New Roles and Relevance: Development NGOs and the Challenge of Change*, eds. David Lewis and Tina Wallace, ix-xvii. Bloomfield, CT: Kumarian Press.

Menchú, Rigoberta (1984), *I, Rigoberta Menchú: An Indian Woman in Guatemala, Edited and introduced by Elisabeth Burgos-Debray, translated by Ann Wright. London: Verso.*

Messer-Davidow, Ellen (2002), *Disciplining Feminisms*, Durham: Duke University Press.

—— (2002), "Feminist Studies and Social Activism," Paper presented at the Feminist Studies Colloquium Series, Department of Women's Studies, University of Minnesota, Minneapolis, USA, September 30.

Mohanty, Chandra Talpade (2003), *Feminism Without Borders: Decolonizing Theory, Practicing Solidarity*, Durham: Duke University Press.

Morgan, Robin, ed. (1984), *Sisterhood is Global: The International Women's Movement Anthology*, New York: Anchor Press.

Moss, Pamela (2002), "Taking On, Thinking About, and Doing Feminist Research in Geography," In *Feminist Geography in Practice: Research and Methods*, ed. Pamela Moss, 1-17, Oxford: Blackwell.

Nagar, Richa (2002), "Footloose Researchers, Traveling Theories and the Politics of Transnational Feminist Praxis," *Gender, Place and Culture* 9:2: 179-186.

Nnaemeka, Obioma (2004), "Nego-Feminism: Theorizing, Practicing and Pruning Africa's Way," *Signs* 29:2: 357-385.

Peake, Linda and D. Alison Trotz (1999), *Gender, Place and Ethnicity*, New York: Routledge.

—— (2001), "Feminism and Feminist Issues in the South." In *The Companion to Development Studies*, eds. V. Desai and R.B. Potter, 34-37. London: Arnold.

Peake, Linda and Audrey Kobayashi (2002), "Policies and Practices for an Anti-racist Geography at the Millennium." *The Professional Geographer* 54:1: 50-61.

Poitevin, Guy (2002), *The Voice and the Will: Subaltern Agency: Forms and Motives*, New Delhi: Manohar.

Pratap, Vijay (1995), "Some Reflections on Funding and Volunteerism," *Lokayan Bulletin* 12:3: 1-4.

Pratt, Geraldine (2004), *Working Feminisms*, Philadelphia: Temple University Press.

Pushpa, Maitreyi (2004), "Baden Laanghti Striyan," *Rashtriya Sahara* [Hindi Daily, New Delhi] March 20: 9.

Rose, Gillian (1997), "Situating Knowledge: Positionality, reflexivities and other tactics" *Progress in Human Geography* 21:3: 305-320.

Roy, Arundhati (2004), "Tide? Or Ivory Snow? Public Power in the Age of Empire." Speech given in San Francisco, California, August 16, Transcript downloaded August 18, 2004 from: http://www.democracynow.org/static/Arundhati_Trans.shtml

Sen, Samita (2002), "Towards a Feminist Politics? The Indian Women's Movement in Historical Perspective," In *The Violence of Development: The Politics of Identity, Gender and Social Inequalities in India*, ed. Karin Kapadia, 459-524, New Delhi: Kali for Women.

Silman, Janet, ed. (1987), *Enough is Enough: Aboriginal Women Speak Out*, Toronto: The Women's Press.

Spivak, Gayatri Chakravorty (2000), "Discussion: An Afterword on the New Subaltern." In *Subaltern Studies XI: Community, Gender, and Violence*, eds. Partha Chatterjee and Pradeep Jeganathan, 305-334. Delhi: Permanent Black and New Delhi: Ravi Dayal Publisher.

Srivastava, Shikha (2004), "Likhna, Aurat ki Zindagi!" *Hindustan*, Adaab Lucknow [Hindi daily, Lucknow] April 1: 1.

Torres, Edén E. (2003), *Chicana Without Apology: The New Chicana Cultural Studies*, New York: Routledge.

Verma, Lal Bahadur (2004), "Tootte Pinjare, Naye Asman," *Vagarth* [Hindi monthly, Kolkata] November: 24-26.

Visweswaran, Kamala (1994), *Fictions of Feminist Ethnography*, Minneapolis: University of Minnesota Press.

Women's Research and Development Project (1991), *Unsung Heroines*, Dar es Salaam: Women's Research and Development Project.